E-BANKING MANAGEMENT

E-BANKING MANAGEMENT

Edited by
Dr. Rabi Narayana Misra
M.Com., LLB., M.Phil, Ph.D.

DISCOVERY PUBLISHING HOUSE PVT. LTD.
NEW DELHI-110 002

Published by:

Namit Wasan

DISCOVERY PUBLISHING HOUSE PVT. LTD.
4383/4B, Ansari Road, Darya Ganj
New Delhi-110 002 (India)
Phone : +91-11-23279245, 43596064-65
Fax : +91-11-23253475
E-mail : discoverypublishinghouse@gmail.com
namitwasan9@gmail.com
sales@discoverypublishinggroup.com
web : www.discoverypublishinggroup.com

***First Edition:* 2016**

ISBN: 978-93-5056-788-3

E-Banking Management

Printed at:
Infinity Imaging Systems
Delhi

Preface

At present banking industry is considered as most important industry not in our country also in the world as whole. Banking sector plays a significant role in development of Indian economy. So, banks need technology to increase penetration, improve their productivity and efficiency deliver cost-effective products and services, provide faster, efficient and convenient customer service and thereby contribute to the overall growth and development of the country.

E-banking refers to Electronic Banking. It is a e-business in banking system to meet the present need of the customers. In this system customers will perform their day-to-day banking transactions in internet system. By this system, bank account informations can be accessed at any time, day or night and at any place. By this system up-to-date informations are to be provided within no time.

Internet banking can also be used on mobile phones. Now-a-days E-banking service very easy and effective. This book is very much helpful to persons dealing with banking services, and business man and executives of companies, students and general public as a whole.

—Dr. Rabi N. Misra

Acknowledgement

I am very much thankful to all paper contributors of this book. It is not possible in my part to edit this book without their help and co-operation.

I am also thankful to my wife Smt. Swarna Prava Misra for her timely help and co-operation for editing this book. My sons Roopesh and Rookesh have provided their helping hands in editing this book, so I am also thankful to them. My elder daughter-in-law Smt. Amrita Rani Misra and younger daughter-in-law Smt. Bandita Misra have also given their timely help in editing this book.

My special thanks to Mr. Tilak Wasan, the Owner/Director of Discovery Publishing House (P) Ltd., New Delhi for publishing this book in time. I have also provided my thanks to his son who is the real leader in publishing this book. At last I would like to thanks all members of publishing division of Discovery Publishing House for help and co-operation in publishing this book in time.

—R.N. Misra

Contents

E-Banking Management
Edited by: Dr. Rabi N. Misra
ISBN: 978-93-5056-788-3
Edition: 2016
Published by: Discovery Publishing House Pvt. Ltd., New Delhi (India)

E-BANKING
A Revolution in Financial Transactions

Prof. R.P. Sarma
Director, Institute of Economic Studies, Brahmapur-760010, Odisha

Introduction

Banking is one of the oldest institutions of the society. There are evidences that bank type institutions were there in Indian Vedic Period in 1750 BC and developed forms of financial transactions in bank type institutions in Mayuriyan Dynastic rule in India (321 - 185 BC). It was the money lenders who were the first bankers; they were lending money on the basis of charging interest on monthly or annual basis mainly by keeping gold ornaments as security. Later they started lending on the mortgage of land or dwellings house.

In middle ages instead of gold coins issued by the kings, the bankers issued written "Notes" for the transfer of funds. When the banks were officially recognized by the state for all types of financial transactions the banks were allowed to issue printed 'notes' for all types of money transactions in different denominations for easy operation of marketing deals. Then the 'Cheque' appeared, which made easy for the large payments. Sending money become easier for all business transactions; the role of the banks has been recognized as vital factor for the economic development of a country.

During the colonial rule, the modern types of banks were established in India. Bank of Hindustan appeared first in 1770 which worked up to 1829. The General Bank of India established in 1786 was also short lived. Bank of Calcutta was established in 1869 changed into several versions and now it is working as State Bank of India. The Bank of Calcutta changed into Bank of Bengal and Bank of Bombay, Bank of Madras. In 20th century all these banks converted into Imperial Bank of India in the year 1921. After independence of India the Imperial Bank of India was converted into State Bank of India which is now the largest commercial bank of the country.

The Revolution

In the second half of twentieth century development of electronics in different uses changed the social and economic aspects of society. Development of satellites, world-wide internet which instantly transfers the voice, picture and letters globally made the social life more enjoyable. It made a sea change in banking. First appeared the ATM, instant money withdrawals easy, one need not go to the bank to get cash from his account. This alone reduced the crowd at the bank almost 75 per cent.

Growth of handy computers, expansion of number of unbelievable mobile phones is now gives more freedom to a bank customer to avail the most important money transactions sitting at home or office, one need not run to a bank for any of his requiems as before. The important facilities are now done in a computer or a mobile phone, more perfectly and quickly. Seven facilities availed by a bank customer by his mobile phone any time during day or night in holidays or working days.

What is E-Banking?

Banking operations through electronic media is termed as E-Banking, it is also known as Internet Banking, Digital Banking or Mobile Banking in different periods and in different countries but now it is popularly known as E-Banking. E-Banking transactions are growing fast in developed countries for daily financial transactions. In recent years from 2004 to 2010 the percentage of people availing E-Banking in Europe increased from 16 per cent to 36 per cent, at the rate of 6 per cent per annum. This is shown in Fig. 1.1.

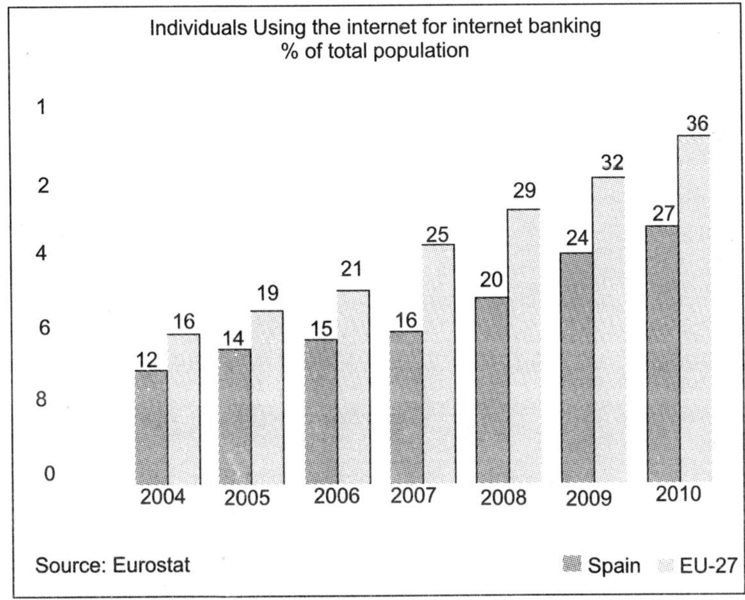

Fig. 1.1 : Growth of E-Banking System in Europe.

E-Banking provides services in a two tier structure: (1) Basic tier and (2) Premium tier. The first tier includes customer account enquiry, funds transfer to other accounts and payment of bill on behalf of the customer. In the second or premier services include numerous other services like brokerage, cash management, credit application, credit and debit cards, customer correspondence, demit holdings, financial advice, foreign exchanging trading, insurance, online trading, tax services, E-shopping, investments, assets management services etc. The seven basic services one gets from E-Banking system is shown in Fig. 1.2 for which a bank customer visits a bank, but now he need not visit a bank for all these transactions; it saves time and cost of travelling to the bank, all these can be down through a PC or a mobile phone sitting at home.

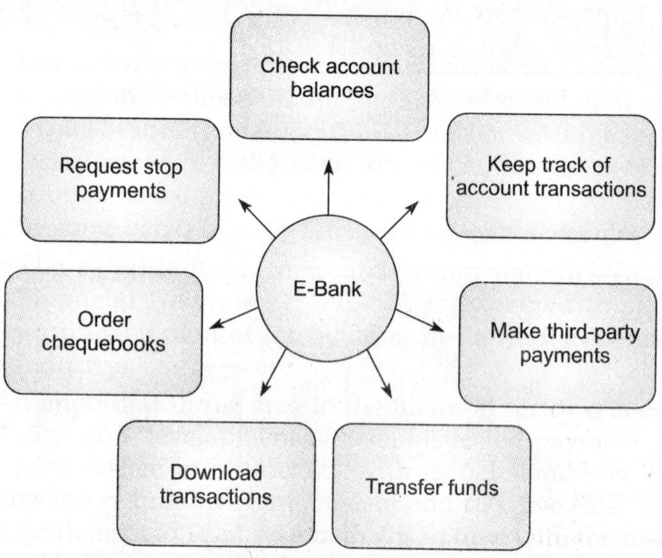

Fig. 1.2 : Basic Services of an E-Bank System

BASIC SERVICES OF E-BANKING

The seven E-Banking services which mostly requires for a bank customers are as follows:

1. Checking of Balance in the Account: A customer can view up-to-the minute balance information on deposits. The customer can also view transaction history with retention period up to a maximum of 90 days. The system will show the View Account page of the customer. One can choose current account or saving account for more details.

2. Keeping Track of Account Transactions: Trasfer Funds allows customer to transfer funds between authorized accounts. Requested transfer take place immediately or at a selected future date specified by customer. The system will display Transfer Funds function for transfer of funds or Transfer History function done.

3. Make Third Party Payments: The customer selects the Bill Payment functionality then the system displays Bill Payments Menu. This function allows a customer to pay Immediate and future payment to corporations, to those customers who have registered. One has to select Corporation Name from the list provided and enters the payment. Amount and bill reference and number will show, if required. The system will display also the Confirm message and show the payment details.

4. Transfer of Funds: Money from one account can be transferred to another account instantly there is no requirement of signing cheques and sending it by post which is time taking.

5. Download of Transactions: The customer can download all transactions from his account during the day and can prepare the plan for the next day operations and prepare his financial plan.

6. Ordering for Cheque Book: One can order for a cheque book on line and the bank sends it by post. One need not visit the bank for this. Of course in E-Banking practically there would be no necessity of a cheque book as money is easily transferred to another account in no time.

7. Requesting the Bank to Stop Payment to Certain Accounts: If the customer wants to withhold payment to a corporation or a person, this also can be done on-line, in E-Banking system. No written application to be submitted to the bank for this.

Apart from these seven services many other services are provided in E-Banking system that helps business sector for quick and efficient operation of their business which helps the economy to grow faster with the use of E-Banking system. Other important benefits to the bank customer through E Banking are can be mentioned here.

Utility Service

Utility allows customer to change password and the secure delivery contact information. Within this feature, the customer can also change the online profile personal information that is retained by the internet banking system only. And the customer can cancel this if he desires.

ATM Facilities

An individual customer no more visits a bank for his requirement of cash, he visits a near-by ATM point for withdrawal of cash. The E-Bank facility helps a customer to change password function and enter new password and IC/Passport No. and update his personal profile.

Fast Changing Scenario

The immediate result of introduction of E-Banking drastically reduced the use of cheques for money transactions as the most of the customers prefer transfer money through electronic method. With the introduction E-Money payments the use of Cheques and cash payments drastically changed in recent years. The E-Money payments in European countries increased

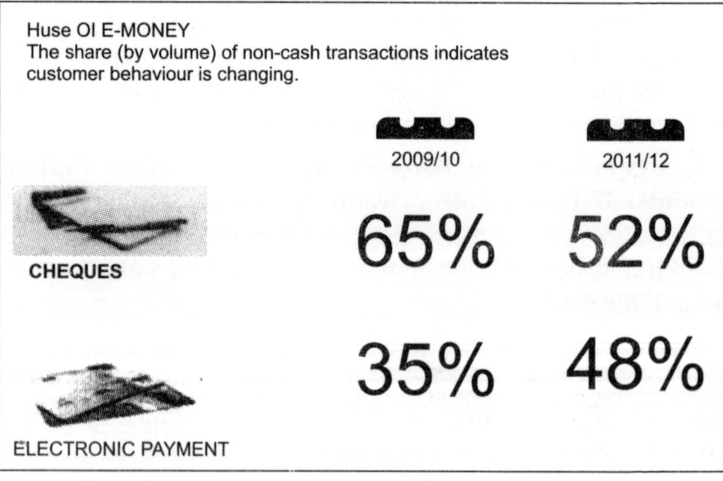

Fig. 1.3 : Changed Money Transactions.

from 35 per cent in 2009-10 to 48 per cent in the year 2011-12. Accordingly the cheque payments reduced 13 per cent from 65 per cent in 2009-10 to 52 per cent in the year 2011-12, as shown in Fig. 1.3.

In the world, the UK banks fast moving in use of E-Banking and it is the first rank in the world followed by USA, Japan and India. In the year 2012 there was 16 per cent growth in the E-Banking activities in UK, followed by 14 per cent in USA, 11 per cent in Japan and 9 per cent in India.

The year-wise growth of E-Banking from the year 2008, 2009, 2010, 2011 and 2012 in the countries of UK, USA, Japan and India is shown in Fig. 1.4.

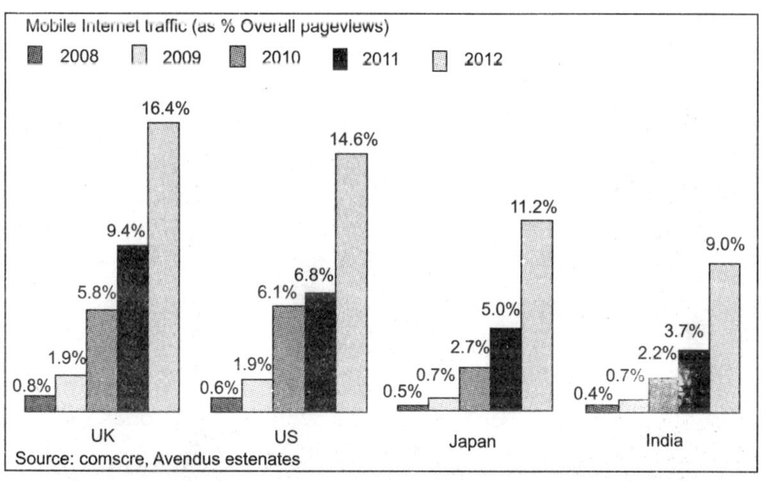

Fig. 1.4 : Growth of Mobile E-Banking System.

Progress in India

In India out of 151 commercial banks, 11 of them introduced E-Banking facilities to the customers. The State Bank of India, the second largest commercial bank of the world is fast to give first the facilities of ATM to its customers. Presently (2013) SBI has 51,753 ATMs throughout India, which is about 31 per cent of all ATMs in the country. This bank has 16,000 branches in India and abroad. In one year from October 2011 to October

2012, E-Bank transactions increased 36.47 per cent which reached 182.71 thousand crores in 2012. The transactions reach peak period in March as that is the last month of financial year in India; the E-Bank transactions reached Rs. 225 thousand crores in March 2012.

Trends of growth of E-Bank transactions of SBI from October 2011 to October 2012 are shown in Fig. 1.5.

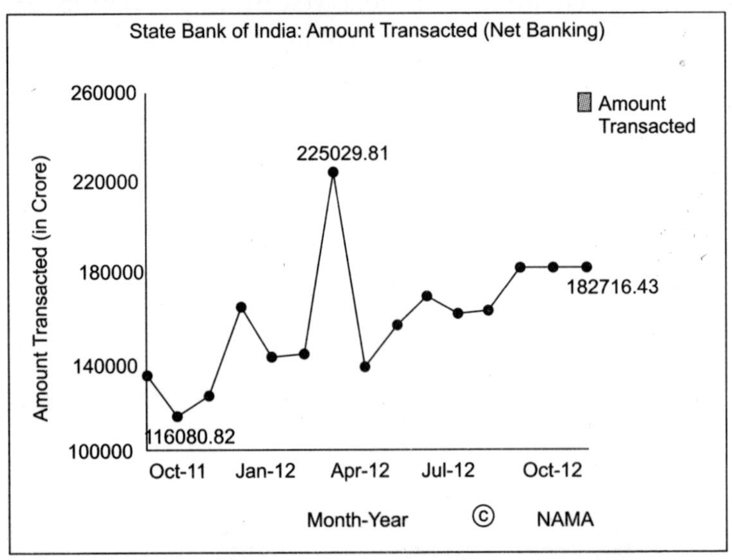

Fig. 1.5 : Growth of SBI Transactions, October to October 2011-12.

Resent trends in mobile banking in India shows that India is fast moving in electronics directions as far as banking is concerned. The number of users increased by 174 per cent from 2011-12 to 2013-14, the volume increased by 271 and value of money increased by 1132 per cent. The figures of users of e-banking, volume and value of money transactions are shown in Table 1.1.

Table 1.1 : Recent Trends in E-Banking in India.

Year	No of Users Million	Volume Million	Value Rs. Billion
2011-12	12.97	25.56	18.21
2012-13	22.51	53.31	59.90
Per cent	73.69	108.56	228.94
2013-14	35.53	94.71	224.38
Per cent	57.84	77.66	274.59

The value and volume of E-Banking transactions in India from 2005-06 to 2013-14 is shown graphically in Fig. 1.6.

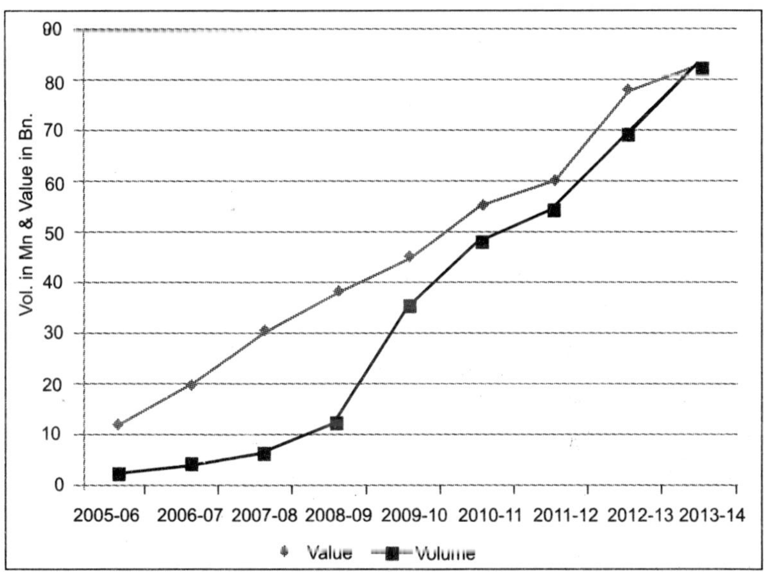

Fig. 1.6 : Value and Volume of Transactions in India through E-Banking.

India is on the path of a digital revolution - it may be ambitious but definitely achievable. Digital Plan of Government of India connecting all the Gram Panchayats through broadband network by 2019 with estimated expenditure of more than 1 trillion are as follows:

1. **Digital infrastructure:** Providing digital identities to people, universal access to bank accounts and phones across the country and safe and secure cyber space.
2. **Governance and services on demand:** On real-time and accessible platform, financial transactions to be electronic and cashless.
3. **Digital empowerment:** All documents and certificates available on cloud. Renewed focus on the National Digital Literacy Mission.

CONCLUSION

E-banking is becoming immensely popular in India. The declining internet and mobile charges, falling prices of PCs and mobile phones, broadband with access through cable and digital subscriber lines etc., would definitely encourage the boom in E-banking in India, it can be concluded that the emerging payment system in India for large value transactions is RTGS, ECS for bulk payments and NEFT for one to one fund transfer move fast. Among the card based payment systems debit card is more popular than credit cards. The number of ATMs in India, particularly in rural areas, is on the rise and customers irrespective of their profile started accepting ATM as a channel for banking transactions, both internet and mobile banking is gaining popularity but considering the rapid penetration of mobile phones in India, the potential for delivering banking services through mobile phones is immense compared to internet as a delivery channel. India will progress ahead with electronic banking in socio-economic sphere in coming decades.

REFERENCES

Deepika Sahdev (2014) A study on Challenges & Opportunities in Indian Banking Sector, Mumbai.

Harun R Khan, (2014) Digital India: Emerging Challenges & Opportunities for the Banking Sector, 16th September, 2014, Reserve Bank of India.

Shamsul Haq1 & Bilal Mustafa Khan (2013) E-Banking Challenges and Opportunities in the Indian Bunking Sector, *Innovative Journal of Business and Management*: July - August, 2013 pp. 56-59.

E-Banking Management
Edited by: Dr. Rabi N. Misra
ISBN: 978-93-5056-788-3
Edition: 2016
Published by: Discovery Publishing House Pvt. Ltd., New Delhi (India)

Internet Banking in Indian Scenario

T. Deepthi
Lecturer in Commerce Department
ASD Government Degree College for Women, Kakinada

Introduction

Banks have traditionally been in the forefront of harnessing technology to improve their products, services and efficiency. The modern age banking customers often transacts through their 'friendly device' that enables them to conduct their bank transactions, trade on the stock exchange, buy their groceries, pay their children's school fee and taxes to the governments through a click of a button. Through their 'friendly device' they open accounts with banks to make the payments, and also carry out transactions at any of the multiple self-service outlets that have been started by their banks.

Today all the above and still more sophisticated services are made available to people through that 'friendly device' called **'Internet'**, which is now identified as ubiquitous communication tool that made its debut in 1983. The Internet is a global web of computer networks, which allowed instantaneous and decentralized global communication possible. Rapid usage of Internet is associated with the development of the user-friendly World Wide Web and web browser software such as Netscape Navigator and Microsoft Internet Explorer.

In the present scenario, most of the business organizations are using the internet for a variety of communication tasks, such as promotion of consumer awareness and interest, providing information and consultation, facilitating two-way communications with customers through e-mail, stimulating product trial and enabling customers to place orders. In order to avail the benefits that are accrued through using Internet, financial institutions like banks are transforming themselves and conducting their business electronically. This transformation from normal banking to electronic banking enabled customers to transact online, while saving on various factors.

Banking through Internet

In the ever changing global scenario, banking business proved to be agile in adopting latest technology to improve its services and efficiency. Banks have evinced interest in delivering value added products and services with the help of rapidly evolving electronic and telecommunication technologies. Amidst these changes, Internet banking evolved in the mid 1990s, i.e., while World Wide Web and internet began to strengthen their roots. Subsequently, dial-up connections, personal computers, tele-banking and Automated Teller Machines (ATMs) became the order of the day in most of the developed countries. Many banking organizations in the US and Europe started providing banking services through Internet.

Internet banking is a web-based service that allows the banks authorized customer to access their account information. In this system, customers are allowed to log on to the bank's website with the help of identification issued by the bank and a Personal Identification Number. Banks replies the user and enables him to access the desired services. Often, the range of products and services offered by each bank on internet varies widely in terms of content. It is observed that Internet banking is offered as a value added service by most of the banks. Owing to the convenience offered by Internet banks, new banks which do not exist physically but conduct their business through Internet have emerged. These are known as 'Virtual Banks' or 'Internet Only' banks.

On the other hand normal banking activities still persist in developing countries like India, where the Internet penetration levels are low. Banking, essentially a service oriented business organization, buys the raw materials or stock-in-trade in the form of deposits and sells the same by way of loans and advances. Hence the bank's functions primarily aim at meeting the saving—credit requirements of a society. But the universal realization in recent years that banks have to play a crucial role in the development process of a country has brought sweeping change both in their organizational as well technical functions, which resulted in Internet banking or e-commerce.

With an aim to be 'customer friendly', Internet bank's products or services are divided into three types:

Information kiosks: It provides information regarding various products and services offered by the bank to its customers apart from other general information. In addition customers' queries are received and answered through e-mail.

Basic Internet Banking: Here, customers are allowed to open new accounts, check account balance and pay utility bills

E-Commerce Banking: Banking transactions are conducted through electronic media, wherein customers are enabled to use their accounts for transferring money, payments of various bills, purchase and sale of securities and online real time purchases and payments. Further, customers banking information is passed from web server to the bank's internet banking service through the WWW interface, to comply with customers requisites. The WWW interface and Internet banking service are significant in Internet banking transaction since they are the only media through which communication is passed from one another, ensuring the safety of operation and customer data. The Internet banking server receives the customers' requests and passes it to the banking server, where the customer database is stored. The database provides the required information to the Internet banking server, which is then passed onto the web server through the fire wall, from where the customer is enabled to access the required information. This type of 'three tiered system', which comprises of web server, Internet banking server and customer database provides a controlled environment and helps in introducing Internet security technologies. There is also a provision for security analyzer that constantly monitors login attempts to log into an account.

Internet banking offers a bundle of benefits to the users who wish to reduce them expenditure on each transaction. According to a study conducted by consultants, Booz Alien & Hamilton, the cost of an average transaction on the Internet is as low as 13 cents, compared to $1.07 through the branch bank 54 cents through the telephone and the 27 cents through the ATM and in India, an Internet banking transaction would cost 10 paise to the bank, as compared to Rs. 1 through a branch, 45 paise through ATM, 35 paise through phone banking and 20 paise through debit cards. Net banking eases transfer of money from one branch in a particular city to another branch in another city. A customer is also further enabled to open a FD account, order for an issue of demand drafts, enquire on the balance in his savings, current and FD account. He is also privileged to give instructions over the net to stop the payment on a cheque, request for a cheque book and verify whether all transactions are completed on his account and get a copy through e-mail.

Net Banks—Global Experience

Globally, banking industry did not remain untouched by the inevitable influence of Internet services. According to a research conducted by-the RBI for Internet services being used by retail banks the world over, it was found that there were over 200 banks with their bank sites on the net, which is shown in the following pie diagram.

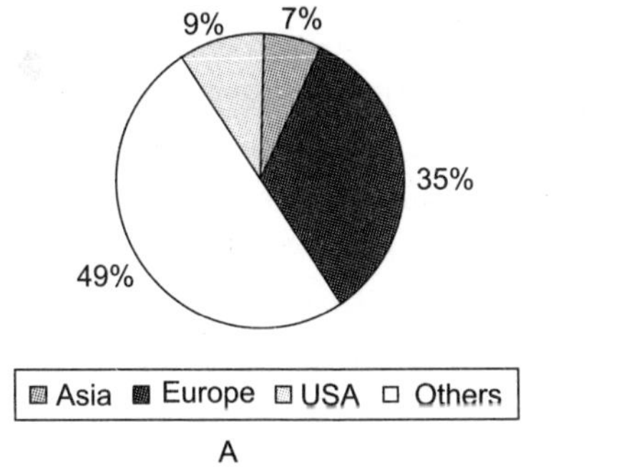

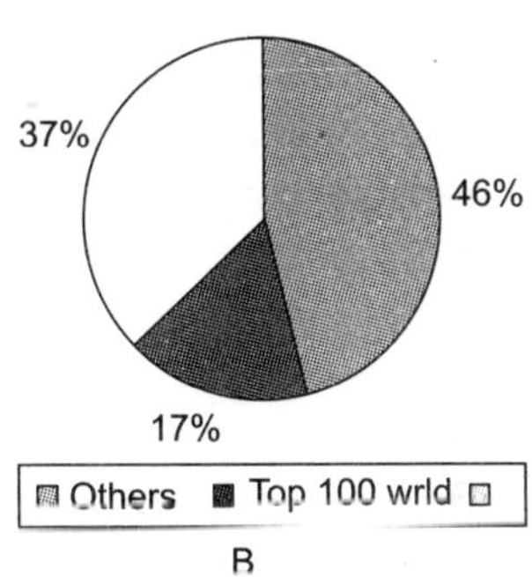

A: Split by geographical region

B: Split by asset strength

The following list of services offered by banks show how online-banking is proved to be lucrative across the world and how valuable web services are becoming to retain the existing customers.

Putting up a Sign: Through this a bank reminds people of its services. It is also called as "maintaining zero presence" by providing information about company head quarters, telephone numbers, company logo etc.

Shop Window: Gives information about banks, its products, annual reports etc. Here interactivity with the customers is absent.

Financial Advice: Banks interact with customers while offering advice services and answering FAQs on wealth allocation and risk tolerance to customers.

Selling Financial Service: Being online, customers are allowed to register, open accounts and fill applications forms for the financial products.

Non-Banking Activities: Banks "off-duty" activities such as charity, welfare and social service are made available on the bank's website.

General Information: A few banks are trying to fulfill the interests of housewives, students, doctors etc. For instance, local banks in America deal with local community news and information; Lloyd's bank provides useful information to the student community.

Virtual Shopping Malls: Banks are trying to convert bank sites to "commerce hubs". Since long time efforts have been made to convert and influence people towards online banking. In this connection, Minitel—a retail banking delivery service, which was developed in France in the early 1980s was the first to be remembered. But today a successful service firm held about sixteen and half million users, which covered 40 per cent of the adult population of the country.

On the other hand, the scenario of Net Banking in India is different, Though a modest attempt to initiate net banking is made, still there is a long way to go. Online banking report 2000, listed features of few banks like ICICI, HDFC, Citi Bank and Global Trust Bank that attempted to make 'real time banking' a reality. In this connection, ICICI bank's net banking service, Infinity offers the following features:

- It allows its customers to transfer funds into another person's account within the bank.
- The customer is enabled to intimate about the loss of an ATM card over the net, while using Infinity.
- Infinity provides a facility to various corporate companies to issue letters of credit and enquire about bills sent for collection.
- "Nicknaming all accounts" is another special feature of infinity which helps to avoid remember lengthy account numbers. Another private sector bank, HDFC Bank enables its customers to have three logins, after which a new password is given. This process ensures safety to the customers. In Global Trust Bank (GTB) the entire back office work is carried out with the help of information technology.

Inward and outward clearing has been centralized. The bank also maintains disaster recovery systems at Hyderabad and Mumbai on 24/7 basis, which ensures 100 per cent uptime. This provision is made apart from the state-of-art e-security to protect safety of all systems from hackers.

UTI bank's Internet banking services offer a wide range of services to the customers like balance enquiry, funds transfer, online trading, e-shopping and e-broking. It is found that the number of hits on the website of the bank exceeds one lakh per day. The bank also provides a bill payment facility through the Internet to its entire internet banking customers. In addition, the bank's web server has been constantly upgraded to meet the anticipated growth in the business.

In spite of rapid efforts to offer net banking facilities, the Indian Internet banking system need to overcome many obstacles, such as operational risks, security risks, system architecture risks, reputational risks and legal risks. Though banks are striving to overcome these problems there is lot to be done towards security of net banking operations. The banks have to be technologically strong to avoid operational and security problems. They should also be prepared to handle system disruptions, system hackers, security lapses and virus attacks. They should also be familiarized with proper customer identification devices, information screening techniques and various laws that would help guide their customers. Thus, with the growing Internet awareness among customers, integration of banking services with e-commerce and entry of global banking players, Internet banking has gained enormous importance. This fact is further proved by RBI guidelines which encouraged the implementation of internet banking in India.

REFERENCES

Aashish Sadh & Soniya Chitale, "Customer Relationship Management & the Banking Industry", Productivity, Vol. 42, No. 1, April—June, 2001.

Banking in the Online World RBR, Internet for the Banking and Financial Service Conference."

GTB Bank Annual Report.

ICICI Bank's Annual Report.

Nath R., M. Akmanligil, K. Hjelm, T. Sakaguchi & T. Schultz (1998), "Electronic Commerce and the Internet: Issues, Problems and Perspectives." International Journal of Information Management 18 (2).

Neela Radhika, "Internet banking in India", E-Business, October 2002.

UTI Bank Annual Report.

Yesil M. "Creating the Virtual Store", crmfoundation.com.

E-Banking Management
Edited by: Dr. Rabi N. Misra
ISBN: 978-93-5056-788-3
Edition: 2016
Published by: Discovery Publishing House Pvt. Ltd., New Delhi (India)

Role of Technology in Banking Services
Trends, Issues and Challenges

Dr. Prem Kumar
Assistant Professor in Commerce
Department of Commerce & Business Management
Vaagdevi Degree & PG College, Hanamkonda

Introduction

Indian economic environment is witnessing path breaking reform measures. The banking industry is the largest player, has also been undergoing a major change. Today the banking industry is stronger and capable of withstanding the pressures of competition. Banking sector plays a significant role in development of Indian economy. So banks need technology to increase penetration, improve their productivity and efficiency, deliver cost-effective products and services, provide faster, efficient and convenient customer service and thereby, contribute to the overall growth and development of the country.

Technology enhances choices, creates new markets, and improves productivity and efficiency. Effective use of technology has a multiplier effect on growth and development. Three aspects should be kept in mind while forming an innovative technology model. First, technology should provide for better customer experience. Second, it should be seamless, easy to use by employees and provide for taking a 360 degree view of the customers. Third, technology adopted should be cost-effective both at the acquisition stage and subsequent operation stage. In the near the future, the Indian banking industry is expected to see consolidation in the wake of future economic growth, changes in banking regulations and increase in competition from foreign banks Technological innovation and especially mobile banking have paved the way for dramatic growth in the industry in the coming years.

The growth story of banking during the last decade has been spectacular and beyond the consistent double digit growth. The key trends were strong regulatory framework, use of multiple channels and technology; strong customer oriented banking services and a growing economy. 2013 promises to be a good year for India. Although a series of challenges like the overall slow down in the economy impacting credit growth, deteriorating asset quality and rising NPAs, accompanying financial inclusion and Basel III implementation are all lingering issues, the sector is well cushioned with factors like a positive demographic dividend, increasing investment in infrastructure, innovation in technology and most importantly constructive regulatory policies.

Objective of the study

1. To review the trends or developments of Technology in Indian Banking Sector.
2. To analyses the impact of Technology in Indian Banking Sector.
3. To suggest various measures for Technological Management.

Methodology

The data have been collected from the secondary sources like various journals, books, Bulletins, and reports of RBI, IBA and other agencies, which are related to the study.

Observations

The paper makes a point that Technology has been a key enabler for banks to transform their business. The role of technology has changed from being a tool to gain operational efficiencies.

Technology in Banking Sector: Historical Perspective

The Rangarajan Committee report in early 1980s was the first step towards computerization of banks. Banks started exploring the idea of 'Total Bank Automation (TBA)'. Although titled Total Bank Automation,' TBA was in most cases confined to branch automation. It was only in the early 1990s that banks started thinking about tying-up disparate branches together to facilitate information sharing.

At the same time, private banks entered the banking arena with radically different strategies. The philosophy for private banks was very clear: to provide a whole new range of financial products and services at minimal costs. The new generation banks showed the way and others had no option but to follow the tech infusion to retain and attract profitable customers.

With centralized infrastructure and numerous connectivity options, banks started exploring. The AAA mantra of anywhere, anytime and anyhow implemented through ATMs, internet banking and mobile banking. The operational costs for transactions through ATMs are comparatively less and also provide flexible options to the customers.

With the establishment of INFFNET (Indian Financial Network) by RBI, using V-SAT technology to provide connectivity of inter-bank and inter-branch has been possible through "Real Time Gross Settlement System". The concept of "bank-customer" has further improved to "banking industry-customer". In this system, the transactions are on real time basis as and when they occurred. Recognizing the need for using IT, the banks have gone for large scale computerization of branches. In contrast, the newer private sector banks have achieved high level of automation and have started offering electronic banking products including Mobile Banking to their top end customers. They have also moved towards electronic banking which include ATMS, shared ATM networks, issue and distribution of plastic cards, tele-banking, on-live submission of loan applications etc.

Today, no banking business or corporate strategy is complete without information technology. So, computerization, information technology and automation of services are key issues for banks to survive in a competitive environment.

It is clear that technology can be used in banking in different ways:

- To handle the expanded customer database.
- To reduce substantially the cost of handling payments.
- To free the bank from traditional constraints on time and place.
- To introduce new products and services to the customers.

Technological latest Innovations–Way forward

"There's only one savior to the Tsunami of competition Innovation".

Indian banking has been consistently working towards the development of technological changes and its usage in its operations. With the application of new and improved technologies banks are expected to reduce costs, time and provide higher customer satisfaction Internet banking or banking via the phone can be considered a remarkable development in the banking industry.

Information Technology has marked a turning point in the history of Indian banking. Technology has opened up new markets, new products, new services and efficient delivery channels for the banking industry. Banks need Technology which is being used to engage customers throughout their lifecycle.

Now time has come for massive adoption and proliferation of new channels—as measured by depth and breadth of usage by customers. New channels will be a primary driver of productivity enhancement in Indian banks in the next decade. Success will depend on initiatives taken by the banks.

Cloud computing: As banks adapt to changing technology environments, cloud computing will play a major role in the next decade. Cloud computing is the IT-based services via the internet. It provides rapid acquisition, low to no capital investment, relatively low operating costs and variable pricing tied directly to use. It accelerates business innovation, facilitates delivery of more personalized services, improves employee productivity and optimises the total cost of technology. However, there is a need for a clear regulatory roadmap to enable the gradual adoption of cloud computing among Indian banks.

Internet-led banking: As the banking system marches ahead on the electronic mode to the hinterland, many micro innovations can take place in providing banking services.

The smart card, bio-metric access to smaller version of ATMs, speaking ATMs and money dispenser can be of great use in the unbanked centres and thus promote financial deepening.

Mobile Banking: India has more than 700 million mobile subscribers, but only 240 million individuals with bank accounts, 20 million credit cards, 88,000 bank branches and 70,000 ATMs. Mobile banking could be a revolution in banking. Over the next five years, unbanked rural markets could begin to rival the urban market in size.

The Internet is widely used by all banking segments around the world to purchase financial services products. It is estimated mobile banking transactions in India will exceed 34 crores in 2015, resulting in cost savings of ₹ 100 crore. After the success of online banking, mobile banking is the next revolutionary step which has attracted huge attention from all over the country. Mobile banking can perform all the banking functions such as money transfer, credit card payment, bill payment, account updates and other transactions.

The banking industry averages about 3 lakh transactions per day through mobile banking and most big banks have seen 100% growth in mobile banking with more services likely to be introduced in the near future. The leading banks in the space are ICICI Bank, HDFC and SBI. Some of the other key players that will join the race in the future include Axis Bank, Syndicate Bank, Canara Bank and Bank of Baroda.

Many customer segments are clearly getting comfortable with using mobile banking. It is particularly true of the Generation-Y group (18—32 year olds) who are three times more likely to adopt mobile banking than older users. Overall the growth in mobile banking that has taken place in the country till date, though at a rapid pace, is yet to reach the critical mass that will enable it to deliver on its promise of taking banking, including payment services, at a cheaper, secure and seamless manner to the existing and potential customers. Banks providing local offers through their mobile banking apps can be a huge value addition and in the next two years banks are expected to leverage on this trend.

Use of 3G technology: Further the advent of 3G in mobile telephony in India will open many avenues for richer service delivery. Priority customers can get 'face to face' financial planning advice on their mobile devices from a set of centrally located advisors.

ATMs-touch points: ATMs are likely to continue to be installed at a rapid pace for the next several years in India. Those banks which have a strategy in place to use ATMs as customer acquisition tools as much as low-cost transaction tools will gain an edge. India has a very low penetration rate of branches and ATMs as compared to some of the other developed and developing nations. The number of ATMs has doubled in the last three years, reaching 99,218 ATMs in June 2012.

The industry is expected to continue this growth and reach 200,0001 ATMs by 2016. As such, most of the new ATMs, 50—65% will be deployed in tier 2 and 3 cities, while tier 1 cities will grow at around 20%.

Future Technological Opportunities and Challenges

The challenge for all banks, large and small, is not only to create a centre of excellence with established international standards of communication, but also to reconstruct and automate their business processes to maximize efficiency. The technology used must be future-proofed to suit integration of existing and future development platforms:

- Growth of the modern, sophisticated and ever-demanding customer.
- Growing population of the "bankable" customers including the youth and the aged.
- Growing prosperity and wealth.
- Increasing number of small and medium sized enterprises.
- Growing interest in new technologies among banks.
- Growth of the modern, sophisticated, technologically skilled perpetrator of crime.

According to a KPMG study, a research analyst says, as of FY 2012, non-cash payments constituted 91 per cent in value terms as compared to 88 per cent in FY in 2010 and 48 per cent in terms of value from 35 per cent in FY 2010. A bank analyst says the payments made through cheques in total non-cash transaction too has come down to 52 per cent from 83 per cent in volume terms, and to nine per cent from 85 per cent in value terms during between FY 2006 and FY 20I2.

Technology Initiatives taken by the Some Banks

- To improve its service quality, SBI has deployed web-based portal where customers can register all kind of complaints. The bank has taken initiatives like dashboards for monitoring of slippages and account tracking centres to keep track on its asset quality. The bank has also implemented updated risk governance structure for integrated risk management which identifies and manages risk at the place of origination itself.

- BoB has taken initiatives like windows server/desktop virtualization and backup consolidation to ensure optimization of resources. The bank has centralized its back office operations including payroll, salary module, electronic tax deducted at source (e-TDS) module and leave module to improve its service delivery and efficiency. For future, the bank has planned initiatives like implementation of business analytics, employee performance management system, employee incentives and manpower planning, advanced phases of customer relationship management and data warehouse, biometric authentication for internal users, etc.
- PNB has done necessary up gradation to make its technology platform more stable, robust and improve quality of assets. During FY2012, the bank has launched various IT-based new products and services like cash deposit machines and self-service passbook printing station to meet the day to day requirement of customers. The bank has established a security operations centre to monitor and analyze threats arising from within the organization. The bank has placed rating/scoring systems at central server network to perform risk analytics.
- Canara Bank has undertaken several technology initiatives like internet banking, mobile banking, online fund transfer, passbook printing self-service kiosk and financial supply chain management facility for corporate customers (for working capital finance).

  During FY 2012, the bank has implemented enterprise-wide data warehouse loaded with business intelligence and analytics for making management decision support system.
- BoI has implemented many technology based customer centric facilities like online nomination facility, banking through mobile service, implementation of school fee module, self-service kiosk, barcode enabled passbook printing, viewing of public provident fund (PPF) account

online and online application for education loans. The bank is also leveraging technology in projects like solar power project, very small aperture terminal (V-sat) connectivity project, credit appraisal processing systems and human resource management system.

- ICICI Bank has leveraged technology to improve customer quality, convenience and reduce customer complaints to enrich customer experience. With the use of internet and mobile banking, the bank has reduced the need for the customers to visit branches. New initiatives like Click Call and 'Your Bank Account' application on Face Book have demonstrated the bank's focus on technology. The bank is also making use of clean technologies to promote sustainable development and to reduce greenhouse gas emissions through energy efficiency.
- Various innovative technology initiatives have helped HDFC Bank to reduce its operating cost, minimize risk and improve customer service quality. HDFC Bank has automated credit underwriting process and has enhanced its cross-selling and up-selling capabilities through the implementation of data mining and analytical customer relationship management solutions. It has enabled the bank to have a 360 degree view of its customers. The bank has adopted six-sigma and lean methodologies to improve its service quality.

  Axis Bank continued to focus on cost-effective technological upgrades to provide improved and timely customer quality. The bank has made significant investments in making scalable and robust technology platform. The bank has launched the business process management system to improve operational efficiencies. Server virtualization and storage centralization have been put in place to ensure optimal utilization of resources.
- KMB implemented technology-driven cash management services to help its customers to simplify and optimize their cash flows and liquidity with efficient working capital cycles.

The bank also continued its focus on information security with enhanced securities in net-banking, emails and data centres.

- IIB's innovations like 'cash-on-mobile', 'direct connect' and 'quick redeem service' have helped the bank in providing better customer satisfaction and increasing its customer base. Using technology in server virtualization, power saving devices and thin computing has helped bank save power consumption and electricity cost. The bank has taken green banking technological initiatives like document management system, e-learning, e-procurement and paperless fax. The bank has also taken several security control measures to enhance its security framework.

The Indian banking sector is experiencing a shift from the traditional branch customer channel to more technology-centric channels. Technology has played an important role in changing the way banks do business or how customers do banking. It has transformed from an enabler to a business driver. Banks need to strengthen their already-built technology platforms to achieve their business objectives. The near future holds an approach of enhanced focus on technology at an accelerating pace.

As rightly summarized by Mr. Anand Sinha, Deputy Governor, RBI, "As we become global, banks would need to become technologically more sophisticated in diverse areas, whether it is moving towards adopting advanced approaches in Basle II or in upgrading their delivery channels for providing better customer service."

Technology a key driver for PSU banks' growth

The public sector banks have seen a technology revolution over a period to provide multiple customer friendly products and services; they are now well placed to offer tremendous career opportunities for youths.

They are also supporting entrepreneurs with a renewed thrust on financing micro, small and medium enterprises

(MSMEs). Indian Bank Executive Director, A Subramanian said, "When more than 100 banks in the US had failed in the wake of global financial meltdown and those in UK were issuing pink slips, it is really creditable for India that none of the scheduled commercial banks have failed. Even those foreign banks, which had failed abroad, are doing well in India". Indian banks are insulated from the worst ever crisis mainly due to the strict control and monitoring by RBI on lending by the banks.

There is a big transformation on the technology front in the banks in the last 30 years. From the days of operating from large premises, handling huge ledgers, followed by partial computerization and operating big ALPM machines, banks have moved to an age of paper-less transactions, ATMs and internet banking facilitated by electronic funds transfer system. A new revolution has come in the form of core banking solutions, which have led to the networking of all the branches of a bank. Instead of a branch customer, one has become a bank customer. Branches or banks are no longer handling deposits and advances. They have become integral part of households enabling them to do any activity or transaction.

Technology has also obviated the need for banks to have a large area for opening branches with more staff. In the past, branches used have a minimum of 1000 sq ft. In the absence of computerisation, not more 100 or 200 accounts could be opened. Now, a branch can handle lakhs of accounts making use of a centralised server located in a secured place. RBI's payment and settlement system called RTGS and anywhere banking concepts have dispensed with the need to take cheques or drafts for fund transfers and remittances.

White-label ATMs

With the Reserve Bank of India (RBI) allowing "white-label" ATMs run by third parties, the number of such machines will increase. That makes the branches relevant only for high-value cash withdrawals and paper-based transactions such as cheque clearing, apart from bulk transactions. The banking system clears some 4-4.5 million cheques a day.

According to analyst estimates, 30—40% of daily transactions are conducted electronically. The latest Reserve Bank of India (RBI) data indicates that electronic payments are on the rise. Outward transactions through RBI's National Electronic Funds Transfer totalled ₹ 18,691 crore in January 2009 with around 3.2 million transactions. In January 2012, there were 20.63 million transactions and the value rose to ₹ .71 trillion—an increase of more than 800% in three years.

HDFC Bank tops the list with 3.01 million transactions, totalling ₹ 23,437.20 crore. SBI comes second with 2.85 million transactions amounting to ₹ 18,393 crore. NEFT is a nationwide payment system to transfer funds from one bank to another. The remitter does not need to send a cheque or demand draft and the beneficiary does not need to visit a bank branch as there is no paper instrument to deposit. "Tech-savvy customers are no longer affected by holidays or strikes. Unless there's a system breakdown, which typically will go unnoticed unless it's a major one and coincides with a strike or a bank holiday, electronic fund transfer has come of age."

CONCLUSION

Indian banking system will further grow in size and complexity while acting as an important agent of economic growth and intermingling different segments of the financial sector. The future of Indian banking depends not only in internal dynamics unleashed by ongoing returns but also on global trends in the financial sectors. With heavy technological adoption in India, it is imperative that the benefits are passed onto the customers at the earliest. It may have to be coerced at the times by way of regulatory norms and at other times through proactive measures as educating the masses about the benefits that would accrue to them.

Technology is the key to move towards providing integrated banking services to customers. Indian banks have been late starter in the adoption of technology for automation of processes and the integrated banking services. But with the global adoption of technology, Indian banking is also at the threshold of paradigm shift due to the latest changes. With the result of such healthy and competitive environment, overall banking system became more work prone, efficient and techno21 savvy.

The transformation in the Indian banking sector, and with the advancement and adoption of technology a lot of changes have been made in payment system and banking system as a whole. Technology is just an instrument to achieve the goal of making banking/financial services available to each and every individual and that too in a very cost effective manner.

Technology should provide for positive return at the quickest possible time. Banks must therefore be wise enough to choose technology which will serve their strategic objective of meeting the competition.

REFRENCES

2 PwC estimates

Dr. Ajay Verma Amita Verma Shodh, Samiksha aur Mulyankan, Emerging Trends in Banking (International Research Journal)—ISSN-0974-2832 Vol. II, Issue-5 (Nov. 08-Jan. 09)

http://rbi.myiris.com

http://www.ibspublishing.com

http://www.rbi.org.in

http://www/bankneti ndia.com

Mishra Sudarshana, "BFSI", PCQUEST, August 2004.

Mittal R. K. and Dhingra Sanjay, "Technology in banking sector: issues and challenges", Vinimay, Vol. XXVII, No. 4, 2006-07

Payment System Vision Document (2012-15) by RBI.

Prof. Jadhav A. S., Mrs. Jadhav R. A., "Status of e-banking in India", National annual convention of CSI2004.

RBI Annual Report, 2011-12 compendium

Source: 1 Celent,The Indian ATM Industry, October 2012

www.economic times.com

www.google.com

www.iba.org.in

E-Banking Management
Edited by: Dr. Rabi N. Misra
ISBN: 978-93-5056-788-3
Edition: 2016
Published by: Discovery Publishing House Pvt. Ltd., New Delhi (India)

Electronic Banking (e-Banking) System

Dr. Braja Mohan Sasmal
Retd. Professor
Seragada Bungalow
Convent School Road
Berhampur-760001

Introduction

Electronic banking or e-banking usually refers to online banking or e-business in banking system. By this system, banking services are delivered through computer controlled internet system. It is a system which allows individuals to perform banking activities sitting before a computer having internet facility, at home. In this system, one need not have to go to a bank and stand in a queue, for banking services. It is a time saving and much quicker system, which avoids physical handling of money.

e-banking or online banking through traditional banks enable customers to perform all routine transactions, such as account transfers, balance enquiries, bill payments, stop payment requests and some even offer online loan and credit card applications. By this system, account information can be accessed at any time, day or night, and can be done from anywhere through computer internet system. A few online banks update information in real time, while others do it daily. Once information has been entered, it does not need to be reentered for similar subsequent checks and future payments can be scheduled to occur automatically.

Some of these services include paying of bills, funds transfer, viewing account statement etc. These banks also deliver their latest products and services over the internet.

Internet banking is performed through a computer system, or similar devices that can connect to the banking site via internet. Now-a-days, you can also use internet banking on your mobile phones using a Wi-Fi or 3G connection. With the ease of availability of cyber cafes in the cities, it has become quite popular in recent years. Banking is now no more limited in going and visiting the bank in person for various purposes. You can do all these tasks and many more other required services using online banking system offered by the banks. You can also keep a track of your account transactions and balance, all the time. Now getting pass books updated to know the total account balance is a matter of past days.

Advantages Of Internet Banking

Internet banking has several advantages over traditional one, which makes operating an account simple and convenient. It allows you to conduct various transactions using the banks website and offers several benefits. Some of the advantages of internet banking are:

1. **Various online services:** Online banking is easy to open and operate. The online services may differ from bank to bank and from country to country. To know about the various services, always go through the welcome kit that you get at the time of opening the account. You also get the pass word to access your online account, which you are supposed to keep secret with care for security of your

account. The common online services offered by banks are:

(*i*) transactional activities like funds transfer, bill payment, loan applications and transactions,

(*ii*) non-transactional activities like request for cheque book, stop payment, online statements updating your contact information.

2. **Convenience:** It is a different task for customers to get time from their busy daily work schedule and visiting a bank during it's working hours only before they close for the day. But by online banking system it is most convenience to get done the banking services simply by logging online whenever it is needed, maybe day or night, and in holidays.
3. **No waiting in a queue:** Generally customers dislike to wait near the counter of a bank in queue wasting their valuable time, which they can use for doing other works. By the help of online banking they can do the banking transactions sitting at home or own office at any time.
4. **Easy availability:** With online banking, you can keep track of your money much easier, because your account information is available at any time. To get your balance, simply login to your account number. You need not wait for the bank to open or to visit an ATM or calling the customer service number. By this system, you can save money and time, as some ATM and customer service call charge a small fee to get your account balance.
5. **Innovative way of handling banking:** By the help of online banking system it is most convenient and innovative way to handle personal finances. Online bill payment, which helps to save time and money. Many online banks also offer the convenience of checking the account information from a cell phone. By this system, one can check the balance by SMS or receive alerts when money is withdrawn or a check clears. Thus, online banking provides better services than a traditional banking system.

6. **Time saving and money saving:** Bill payments and funds transfer are less expensive when you pay with e-banking. Online banking service is always free if you have any one of the customer packages such as; finance transactions, checking accounts, checking balance and transfer funds, renewing the accounts record of last 13 months, bill payments day and night, setting up savings, and deposit accounts, transfer of funds internationally, receiving text or e-mail alerts advising you when your salary has been deposited into your account or passing of the balances after a certain level, setting up or cancelling the standing orders, trade stocks and shares on up to 13 global stock exchanges etc.
7. **Fast and efficient:** Through online banking, funds get transferred from one account to the other, very fast several accounts can also be managed easily through internet banking.
8. **Safe banking:** Through internet tracking you can keep an eye on your transactions and account balance all the time. This facility also keeps your account safe. Due to the ease of monitoring your accounts at any time, you can get to know about any fraudulent activity or threat to your account, before it can pose your account to severe damage.
9. **Better medium:** It also acts as a better medium for the banks to endorse their products and services. The services include loans, investment options and many others.

Disadvantages of Internet Banking

Online banking has some disadvantages, which must be taken care of for achieving better service. The disadvantages of online banking are as mentioned below:

In this system setting up an account may take time in order to register for your banks online program, you will probably have to provide ID and sign a form at a bank branch some banks even ask for photos.

For small business, online banking may have several disadvantages. Modem age of computer and internet provides additional ways to conduct everyday transactions, including banking. But for small business, online banking offers advantages like accessing funds 24 hours a day or saving time by making a few visits to the bank.

1. **Difficulty in accessibility:** If a business is located in a rural or remote area your internet options could be limited. Depending on the type of business, this can make a conducting transactions difficult. Take the example of home based business, which do not have access to a high speed cable connection, may have to use a slower dial-up service. As such the business banking may take more time or it might even experience times, where it can get online:
   (*a*) Understanding of the usage of internet banking might be difficult for a beginner at the first go. Though there are some sites which offer a demo on how to access on line accounts, but not all banks offer this facilities. So, a person or businessman who is new might face some difficulty.
   (*b*) You cannot have access to online banking if you do not have an internet connection thus without the availability of internet access, it may not be useful.
   (*c*) Security of transactions is a big issue. Your account information might get hacked by unauthorized people over the internet. Further password security is a must. After receiving your password, do change it and memorize it, otherwise your account maybe misused by some one who gets to know your password easily.
   (*d*) Another most important issue is that sometimes it becomes difficult to note whether your transaction was successful or not. It may be due to the loss of net connectivity in between or due to a slow connection, or the banks server is down.
2. **Site disruptions:** A technical difficulty could cause the bank website to got offline for a period of time, possibly

resulting in problems for you and your business. For example you may need immediate funds after normal banking hours to make a payment or emergency business purchase. Routine site maintenance also occurs, although this normally takes place during off-peak hours of the day.

3. **Site navigating:** If you are new to online banking, it may take some time to get used to it, taking valuable time out of your working day. Online banking offers a large number of transactions, so frustration may occur while you are learning to navigate the site. Sometimes, banks also update web pages to add new features, requiring additional learning and possibly the need to change account numbers or passwords. If you would help, you might encounter a lengthy waiting when using the bank's telephone, customer service line.

CONCLUSION

However, internet banking has definitely made the life much more easy for users by providing online access to various banking services at any place, any time, and any day as per one's wish.

E-Banking Management
Edited by: Dr. Rabi N. Misra
ISBN: 978-93-5056-788-3
Edition: 2016
Published by: Discovery Publishing House Pvt. Ltd.,
New Delhi (India)

Internet Banking a Boon or Bane to Indian Banking Sector

R. Meena Kumari
Lecturer in Commerce,
Government Degree College for Women,
Sangareddy-502001, Medak Dist.

Introduction

Today, Indian banks are working under intense competitions from new generation banks and foreign banks. Banks are embracing new and cost effective delivery channel. Offering attractive value added services is the only way to retain and attract the customers. Technology plays a major role in the development of alternate channels and interactions between customers and banks. Performances of Commercial Banks were improved after the introduction of IT Act, 1999. The internet is revolutionizing the banking industry to conduct its business through online familiarly called as Internet banking or online banking. It offers personalized services through the web portals. Internet banking involves use of Internet for delivery of banking products & services. It provides enormous benefits to consumers like access his accounts at anytime and from any location with ease and least cost.

Internet banking became a boon to Indian banking industry to retain customers in heavy competition. But on the other side it became bane by facing electronic frauds like phishing etc.

Objective of the Study

- To know whether internet banking is a boon or bane for the banking industry.
- To study the challenges and opportunities for all banks by e-banking.

Scope of the Study

Traditional branch based retail banking remains the most wide spread method for banking transaction. However the internet technology rapidly changing the way of designing and delivering the services. There is a need to understand the advantages and disadvantages of it and take the measures to improve the usage of internet banking.

What is Internet Banking

Internet Banking refers to the banking services provided by the banks over the internet. Some of these services include paying of bills, funds transfer, viewing account statement, etc. Banks also deliver their latest products and services over the internet. Banking is now no more limited in going and visiting the bank in person for various purposes like depositing and withdrawing money, requesting for account statement, stop a payment, etc.

Services Offered by Online Banking

Internet banking account is easy to open and operate. The services offered by banks over the internet might differ from bank to bank, and from country to country.

The common **internet banking services** offered by banks are:

- **Transactional activities** like funds transfer, bill pay, loan applications and transactions.

- **Non-transactional activities** like request for cheque book, stop payment, online statements, updating our contact information.

Remote banking **does not provide** the following services:

- Cash withdrawals;
- Cash/cheque deposit;
- Sale of the more complex types of financial services such as life insurance mortgages and pensions.

Advantages of Internet Banking

Internet Banking has several advantages over traditional banking which makes operating a bank account simple and convenient. Internet banking allows us to conduct various transactions using the bank's website and offers several advantages. Some of the advantages of internet banking are:

- Internet banking account is simple to open and easy to operate.
- Internet banking is quite convenient as we can easily pay our bills, can transfer funds between accounts, etc. Now we do not have to stand in a queue to pay off our bills; also we do not have to keep receipts of all the bills as we can now easily view our transactions.
- Internet banking is available all the time, i.e. 24 × 7. We can perform our tasks from anywhere and at any time; even in night when the bank is closed or on holidays. The only thing you need to have is an internet connection.
- Internet banking is fast and efficient. Funds get transferred from one account to the other very fast. We can also manage several accounts easily through internet banking.
- Through Internet banking, we can keep an eye on our transactions and account balance all the time. This facility also keeps our account safe. This means that by the ease of monitoring our account at anytime, we can get to know about any fraudulent activity or threat to our account before it can pose our account to severe damage.

- Internet banking is also a great medium for the banks to endorse their products and services. The services include loans, investment options, and many others.

Disadvantages of Internet Banking

Though there are many advantages of internet banking, but nothing comes without disadvantages and.everything has its pros and cons; same is with internet banking. It also has some disadvantages which must be taken care of. The disadvantages of internet banking include the following:

- Understanding the usage of internet banking might be difficult for a beginner at the first go. Though there are some sites which offer a demo on how to use internet banking, but all does not offer this facility. So, a person who is new to internet baking might face some difficulty.
- We cannot have access to internet banking if we don't have an internet connection; thus without the availability of internet access, internet banking may not be useful.
- **Password security** is a must. After getting our net banking password, do change it and memorize it otherwise our account may be misused by someone who gets to know our password inadvertently.

  We cannot use internet banking, in case, the bank's server is down.
- Another issue is that sometimes it becomes difficult to note whether our transaction was successful or not. It may be due to the loss of internet connectivity in between, or due to a slow connection, or the bank's server is down.
- **Security of transactions is a big issue. Our account information might get hacked by unauthorized people over the internet, which is called phishing.**

What is Phishing

Phishing is a form of Internet fraud in which criminals create a fake copy of a popular site (an email service, an Internet banking website, a social networking site, etc.) and try to attract the users to these web pages. The unsuspecting user enters their login information and passwords into these carefully forged websites as they normally would, but these access credentials are instead sent to the cyber criminals. The scammers can then use this stolen personal information, bank credentials, or passwords to steal the users' money, to distribute spam and malware via the compromised email or social networking accounts, or they can simply sell their databases of stolen passwords to other criminals.

Main Research Findings *(Retrieved from Kaspersky Research)*

Users

- In 2012-2013, phishers launched attacks affecting an average of 102,100 people worldwide each day - twice as many as in 2011-2012.
- Phishing attacks most often target users in Russia, the USA, India, Vietnam and the UK.
- Vietnam, the USA, India and Germany have the greatest number of attacked users—the total number of attacks in these regions has doubled since last-year.

Attackers

- The majority of the servers hosting phishing pages were registered in the USA, the UK, Germany, Russia and India.
- The number of unique attack sources - such as fraudulent websites and servers - has more than tripled from 2012-2013.
- Over half (56%) of all identified unique attack sources were found in just 10 countries, which means the attackers have a small set of preferred "home bases" to launch their attacks.

Targets

- The services of Yahoo!, Google, Facebook and Amazon were most often attacked by phishers—30% of all registered incidents involved fake versions of their sites.

- Over 20% of all phishing attacks mimicked banks and other financial organizations.

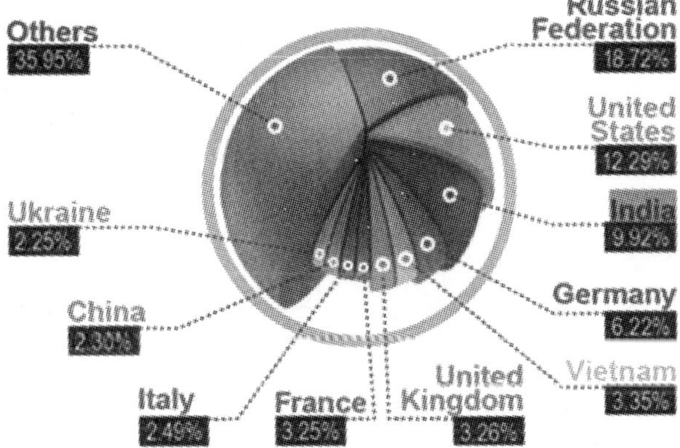

Fig. 5.1: Top 10 attacked countries in 2012-13.

Source: Kaspersky phishing Reports.

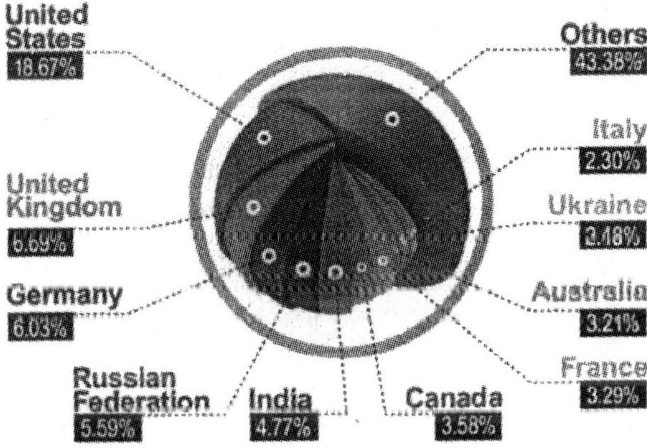

Fig. 5.2: Most of the Pishing Attacks are Coming From.

Source: Kapersky phishing Report.

Table 5.1: Technology Related Frauds at Banks for the last 4 years.

Bank Group-wise Technology Related Frauds

(No. of cases in absolute terms and amount involved in Rs. Crore)

Bank Group	2009-10		2010-11		2011-12		2012-13		Cumulative total (As at end March 2013)	
	No. of cases	Amount involved	No. of cases	Amount involved	No. of cases	Amount involved	No. of cases	Amount involved	No. of cases	Amount Involved
Nationalized Banks including SBI Group	118	1.82	143	3.39	172	7.26	190	9.85	824	25.60
Old Private Sector Banks	9	0.15	4	0.46	9	0.06	6	1.09	55	2.30
New Private Sector Banks	14387	34.53	9638	21.41	6552	16.54	3408	33.97	74321	183.48
Sub Total	14396	34.68	9642	21.87	6561	16.6	3414	35.06	75200	211.38
Foreign Banks	5273	26.83	4486	14.77	3315	14.60	5161	22.45	36455	145.95
Grand Total	19787	63.38	14271	40.03	10048	38.46	8765	67.36	111655	357.33

Source : www.rbi.org.in

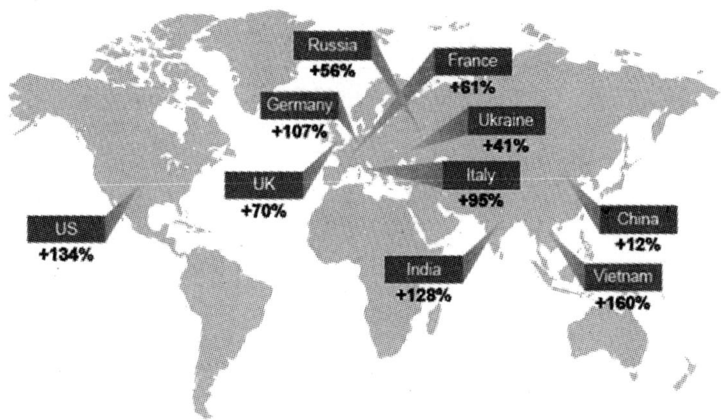

Fig. 5.3: Top 10 Countries highest growth rate in the phishing attacks

Source: Kaspersky Phishing Report.

CONCLUSION

The present study is an attempt to present the status of internet banking in India and its implications for Indian banking industry. The introduction of internet banking has helped the financial institutions to cope with new economic and financial policies of the banks. Internet banking is on rise and it becomes a powerful tool for improving customer satisfaction and increasing cross-selling opportunities. At the same time internet banking has its pitfalls too. There are a number of challenges which banks must keep in mind. Financial institutions must do more to protect themselves and their customers from ongoing phishing attacks and data breaches. They must ensure that consumers feel safe when using online banking features, keeping track of ever changing banking industry and the latest update in internet technology, banks need to equip themselves for the competition. And many results show that security and privacy, trust, innovativeness, familiarity and awareness have positive influence on the acceptance of e-banking services in India. Education campaigns have some impact on spear-phishing awareness. Banks should increase the level of awareness and should kept their promises and commitment.

REFERENCES

Bank Phishing Scam. Retrieved from http://www.phishing.org/scams/bank-phishing/

K.C.Chakrabarthy, Deputy Governor, Reserve Bank of India (Speech on Inaugural Address on July 26th, 2013) Frauds in the Banking Sector: Causes, Concerns & Cures Retrieved from http://www.rbi.org.in/scripts/BS SpeechesView,aspx?Id=826

Kaspersky Lab : The Evaluation of Phishing Attacks 2011-2013. Retrieved from http://media.kaspersky.com/pdf/Kaspersky Lab KSN report. The Evolution of Phishing Attac ks 2011-2013.pdf

Monika Kashyap & Dr.Dinesh Kumar Sharma (2012). Internet Banking Boon or Bane. Gian Jyothi E-Journal Volume 1, Issue 2 (Jan. - Mar 2012).

Neha Dixit (Aug, 2010). Acceptance of E-banking among Adult Customer: An Imperical Investigation in India. Journal of Internet banking and Commerce.

Tracy Kitten (July 22nd, 2013) Spear-Phishing: What Banks Must Do. Retrieved from http://www.bankinfosecuritv.in/spear-phishing-what-banks-must-do -a-5923

E-Banking Management
Edited by: Dr. Rabi N. Misra
ISBN: 978-93-5056-788-3
Edition: 2016
Published by: Discovery Publishing House Pvt. Ltd.,
New Delhi (India)

Role of Information Technology in Banking Sector with Reference to India

M. Rambabu
Lecturer in Economics,
SAS Government Degree College
Narayanapuram
West Godavari Dist.

Introduction

Technology has brought a complete paradigm shift in the functioning of banks and delivery of banking services. Gone are the days when every banking transaction required a visit to the bank branch. Today, most of the transactions can be done from the home and customers need not visit the bank branch for anything. Technology is no longer an enabler, but a business driver. The growth of the internet, mobiles and communication technology has added a different dimension to banking. The information technology (IT) available today is being leveraged in customer acquisitions, driving automation and process efficiency, delivering ease and efficiency to customers. With the globalization trends world over it is difficult for any nation big or small, developed or developing, to remain isolated from what is happening around. For a country like

India, which is one of the most promising emerging markets, such isolation is nearly impossible. More particularly in the area of Information Technology, where India has definitely an edge over its competitors, remaining away or uniformity of the world trends is untenable. Over the last three decades, there has been a phenomenal increase in the size, spread, and activities undertaken by banks in India. From approximately 8,000 bank branches in 1969, the number has now reached over 64,000.

Need and importance of the study

The very need of present study is to find the role of Information Technology in Banking Sector in the globalization era. We have aimed to know the role of Information Technology in Banking Sector.

Objectives of the study

The main objectives of our present paper are:

- To study the growth of Information Technology;
- To observe recent trends in Banking Sector;
- To identify the role of Information Technology in Indian Banking Sector.

Methodology

The present study is based on the secondary data published by various agencies and organization, necessary secondary data on conceptual framework and review of literature are collected from journals, magazines, periodicals and other publications.

Growth and expansion

Over the last Decade, the size of the banking industry has grown by 7.5 times. The business per employee has increased from INR 27.6 million in 2005-06 to INR 62.7 million in 2009-10, while the profit per employee increased from INR 0.12 million in 2005-06 to INR 0.39 million in 2009-10. Indian banks are also no longer constrained by geography as they have worldwide operations. IT has been instrumental in the global expansion of banks. It is a huge challenge for banks to maintain and keep the vast network operational. IT has helped banks put in place alternate delivery channels such as internet and phone. Mobile banking and ATMs are rapidly becoming the prime delivery channels. The consolidation and centralization of information is also providing banks with accelerated decision-making and risk management capabilities. Electronic payments through credit and debit cards are also emerging as a fast-growing segment providing ease of use and convenience to customers.

Trends in Information Technology

Certain trends have been visualized of information technology in banking sector all over the world:

(1) Outsourcing: Outsourcing is one of the most talked about as also a controversial issue. The drivers for getting in to outsourcing are many to include gaps in IT expectations and the reality, demystification of computerization in general and IT in particulars, trend towards focusing on core competencies, increased legitimacy of outsourcing and intention of getting out of worries and sort of upgradation of hardware and software versions. Not that the practice is new as earlier it was refused to as 'buying time' or 'service bureau'. What is needed is the clear of outsourcing, beside a definite plan to be more competitive after outsourcing. It is necessary to have checks and balances to monitor vendor performance. Cost aspects merit consideration, as also a decision on the part of the process to be outsourced shall be significance. Exit route and resource on the amount of failure after outsourcing are the other issue to be looked onto. Notwithstanding these risks, outsourcing has come to say.

(2) Integration: One of the IT trend is moving from hierarchy to team approach. The purpose is to see an alternative to retooling, to react speedily and to develop capabilities rather than exploiting them. Such integration is necessary so as to address to prevalent situations.

(3) From Solo to Partnership: With the development of IT, two things are taking place simultaneously. The work force as a percentage of total staff is going down and spending on IT as percentage of total spending is going up. The forms of partnership can include binding by superior service, accommodation in service sharing network, equal partnership and situations, where survival is threatened.

(4) IT as Profit Centre: In the embryonic phases, IT was looked upon a means to get rid of high processing cost and time and to convert the manual operation with high volume/ low complexity in two mechanical ones. With the evolutionary the process, it was seen as the best means of generating, MIS. The same approach gave the status of DSS to IT. All along, IT has been recognized as the service function in Indian Banks. However, the new trend that is emerging is considering IT as a profit centre.

(5) Prospering in Down Market: The trend suggests that when there is a down turn in the market place, Pro-active corporations take the benefit of available unutilized resources to upgrade and revisit technology issues. This is seen as the right time to establish the R & D centre for IT. There are false notions about technology and its capability. Some misconceptions include:

- Best-fit possible technology is implemented.
- System solution is good enough and there is need to look into user expectations.
- Innovations are generally successful.
- Success is related only to novel ideas.

(6) Leading to Downsizing: The IT initiative is making the organization lean and flat. For IT functionaries downsizing means transferring computing power from mainframe to the personal computer and workstations. Downsizing is a typical issue faced with associated problems. Absence of top management commitment, lack of understanding of the prevalent IT infrastructure, doing too much and too fast and undertaking the exercise without a framework for controlling the downsizing operations are primarily the situations that create adversities in downsizing. In any case the trend of downsizing is very much existent in the IT environment

(7) Getting Competitive Intelligence: IT is now seen as a resource for gathering and dissemination of executive information system (EIS). The purpose is to minimize that the bombarding and focusing on the relevance, accuracy and timeliness of the information particularly about the competitors such information enhances follow up and tracks early warning on competitor move and also customer expectations.

Recent Developments in Banking Sector

1. Internet: Internet is a networking of computers. In this marketing message can be transferred and received worldwide. The data can be sent and received in any part of the world. In no time, internet facility can do many a job for us. It includes the following:

- This net can work as electronic mailing system.
- It can have access to the distant database, which may be a newspaper of foreign country.
- We can exchange our ideas through Internet. We can make contact with anyone who is a linked with internet.
- On internet, we can exchange letters, figures/diagrams and music recording. Internet is a fast developing net and is of utmost important for public sector undertaking, Education Institutions, Research Organization etc.

2. Society for Worldwide Inter-bank Financial Telecommunications (SWIFT): SWIFT, as a co-operative society was formed in May 1973 with 239 participating banks from 15 countries with its headquarters at Brussels. It started functioning in May 1977. RBI and 27 other public sector banks as well as 8 foreign banks in India have obtained the membership of the SWIFT. SWIFT provides have rapid, secure, reliable and cost effective mode of transmitting the financial messages worldwide. At present more than 3000 banks are the members of the network. To cater to the growth in messages, SWIFT was upgrade in the 80s and this version is called SWIFT-II. Banks in India are hooked to SWIFT-II system. SWIFT is a method of the sophisticated message transmission of international repute.

This is highly cost effective, reliable and safe means of fund transfer:

- This network also facilitates the transfer of messages relating to fixed deposit, interest payment, debit-credit statements, foreign exchange etc.
- This service is available throughout the year, 24 hours a day.
- This system ensure against any loss of mutilation against transmission.
- It serves almost all financial institution and selected range of other users.

It is clear from the above benefit of SWIFT that it is very beneficial in effective customer service. SWIFT has extended its range to users like brokers, trust and other agents.

3. Electronic Payment Services-E Cheques: Now-a-days we are hearing about e-governance, e-mail, e-commerce, e-tail etc. In the same manner, a new technology is being developed in US for introduction of e-cheque, which will eventually replace the conventional paper cheque. India, as harbinger to the introduction of e-cheque, the Negotiable Instruments Act has already been amended to include; Truncated cheque and E-cheque instruments.

4. Real Time Gross Settlement (RTGS): Real Time Gross Settlement system, introduced in India since March 2004, is a Interlink Research Analysis system through which electronics instructions can be given by banks to transfer funds from their account to the account of another bank. The (RTGS) Real Time "Gross Settlement system is maintained and operated by the RBI and provides a means of efficient and faster funds transfer among banks facilitating their financial operations. As the name suggests, funds transfer between banks takes place o a 'Real Time' basis. Therefore, money can reach the beneficiary instantaneously and the beneficiary's bank has the responsibility to credit the beneficiary's account within two hours.

5. Automatic Teller Machine (ATM): Automatic Teller Machine is the most popular devise in India, which enables the customers to withdraw their money 24 hours a day 7 days a week. It is a device that allows customer who has an Automatic Teller Machine (ATM) card to perform routine banking transactions without interacting with a human teller. In addition to cash withdrawal, Automatic Teller Machines (ATMs) can be used for payment of utility bills, funds transfer between accounts, deposit of cheques and cash into accounts, balance enquiry etc.

6. Point of Sale Terminal: Point of Sale Terminal is a computer terminal that is linked online to the computerized customer information files in a bank and magnetically encoded plastic transaction card that identifies the customer to the computer. During a transaction, the customer's account is debited and the retailer's account is credited by the computer for the amount of purchase.

7. Tele Banking: Tele Banking facilitates the customer to do entire non-cash related banking on telephone. Under this devise Automatic Voice Recorder is used for simpler queries and transactions. For complicated queries and transactions, manned phone terminals are used.

8. Electronic Data Interchange (EDI): Electronic Data Interchange is the electronic exchange of business documents like purchase order, invoices, shipping notices, receiving advices etc., in a standard, computer processed, universally accepted format between trading partners. Electronic Data Interchange (EDI) can also be used to transmit financial information and payments in electronic form.

9. Chip Card: The customer of the bank is provided with a special type of credit card which bears customer's name, code etc. The credit amount of the customer account is written on the card with magnetic methods. The computer can read these magnetic spots. When the customer uses this card, the credit amount written on the card starts decreasing. After use of number of times, at one stage, the balance becomes nil on the card. At that juncture, the card is of no use. The customer has to deposit cash in his account for re-use of the card. Again the credit amount is written on the card by magnetic means.

10. Phone Banking: Customers can now dial up the bank's designed telephone number and he by dialing his ID number will be able to get connectivity to bank's designated computer. The software provided in the machine interactive with the computer asking him to dial the code number of service required by him and suitably answers him. By using Automatic voice recorder (AYR) for simple queries and transactions and manned phone terminals for complicated queries and transactions, the customer can actually do entire non-cash relating banking on telephone: Anywhere, Anytime.

11. Cash Dispensers: Cash withdrawal is the basic service rendered by the bank branches. The cash payment is made by the cashier or teller of the cash dispenses is an alternate to time saving. The operations by this machine are cheaper than manual operations and this machine is cheaper and fast than that of ATM. The customer is provided with a plastic card, which is magnetically coated. After completing the formalities, the machine allows the machine the transactions for required amount.

12. Internet Banking: Internet banking enables a customer to do banking transactions through the bank's website on the Internet. It is a system of accessing accounts and general information on bank products and services through a computer while sitting in its office or home. This is also called virtual banking. It is more or less bringing the bank to your computer. In traditional banking one has to approach the branch in person, to withdraw cash or deposit a cheque or request a statement of accounts etc., but internet banking has changed the way of banking. Now one can operate all these type of transactions on his computer through website of bank. All such transactions are encrypted; using sophisticated multi-layered security architecture, including firewalls and filters. One can be rest assured that one's transactions are secure and confidential.

13. Mobile Banking: Mobile banking facility is an extension of internet banking. The bank is in association with the cellular service providers offers this service. For this service, mobile phone should either be SMS or WAP enabled. These facilities are available even to those customers with only credit card accounts with the bank.

14. Any where Banking: With expansion of technology, it is now possible to obtain financial details from the bank from remote locations. Basic transaction can be effected from far-a-way places. Automated Teller Machines are playing an important role in providing remote services to the customers. Withdrawals from other stations have been possible due to inter-station connectivity of ATM's. The Rangarajan committee had also suggested the installation of ATM at non-branch locations, airports, hotels, Railway Stations, Office Computers, Remote Banking is being further extended to the customer's office and home.

15. Voice Mail: Talking of answering systems, there are several banks mainly foreign banks now offering very advanced touch tone telephone answering service which route the customer call directly to the department concerned and allow the customer to leave a message for the concerned desk or department, if the person is not available.

Challenges in Implementation

It is becoming increasingly imperative for banks to assess and ascertain the benefits of technology implementation. The fruits of technology will certainly taste a lot sweeter when the returns can be measured in absolute terms, but it needs precautions and the safety nets. The increasing use of technology in banks has also brought up 'security' concerns. To avoid any mishaps on this account, banks ought to have in place a well-documented security policy including network security and internal security. The passing of the Information Technology

Act, 2000 has come as a boon to the banking sector, and banks should now ensure to abide strictly by its covenants. An effort should also be made to cover e-business in the country's consumer laws.

Important Business Challenges

- Meet customer expectations on service and facility offered by the bank.
- Customer retention.
- Managing the spread and sustain the operating profit.
- Retaining the current market share in the industry and the improving the same.
- Completion from other players in the banking industry.

Other Important Operational Challenges

- Frequent challenges in technologies used focusing up grades in hardware and software, attending to that implementation issues and timely roll out.
- Managing technology, security and business risks.
- System re-engineering to enable. Defined and implemented efficient processes to be able to reap benefits off technology to its fullest potential.
- Upgrading the skill of workforce spread across the country.

CONCLUSION

Indian public sector banks that hold around 75 % of market share do have taken initiative in the field of IT. They are moving towards the centralized database and decentralize decisions-making process. They posses enviable quality manpower. Awareness and appreciation of IT are very much there. What is needed is a 'big push' the way it was given in the post-nationalization period for expansionary activities. From enabling banking services to driving transformation in the Industry. Information Technology course do promise to change the pace of banking to the next few years. Mobile bank and internet banking are going to make indoor in the banking sector in the near future. Even though IT systems are complex and sophisticated but they are "energy guzzlers". Hence, the future for banking sector is going to make rapid straights in near future As far as banking industry in India is concerned it can be said that although the Indian banks may not be as technologically advanced as their counterparts in the developed world, they are following the majority of international trends on the IT front. The strength of Indian banking lie in withering storms and rising up to the expectations from all the quarters-catching up with all the global trends is a matter of time.

REFERENCES

Arvind Sharma, "IT in Banking - Promise of More Benefits, The Hindu Survey of Indian Industry-2007, pp. 54-58.

Bakshi, S., 'Corporate Governance in Transformation Times', IBA Bulletin, 2003.

Bimil Jalan, "Strengthening Indian Banking and Finance- Progress and Prospects", The Bank Economist Conference, India, 2002.

Biswas, S (1997). "Information Technology in Service Sector - A Vision for India," Information Today and Tomorrow, Vol. 16, No. 3, pp 5-8.

Cash, JI; McFarlan, WE; McKenny, JL and Vital, MR (1988). Corporate Information Systems Management: Texts and Cases, Illinois: Irwin, Homewood.

Mariappan V, "Changing the Way of Baning in India : Technology as a Driver — What is the Trigger?", Vinimaya, Vol. XXVI, No. 2, July-September, pp. 26-34, 2005.

Mittal R.K, Dhingra Sanjay, "Technology in Banking Sector: Issues and Challenges", Vinimaya, Vol. XXVII, No. 4, Jan. March, 2007, pp 14-22, 2007.

Reddy, Y.V. (2000), Monetary and Financial Sector Reforms in India, A Central Banker's Perspective, UBS Publishers, New Delhi.

Reserve Bank of India (1991) Report of the Committee on the Financial System (Chairman Shri M.Narasimham).

Sathish.D, Bala Bharathi. Y", Indian Banking Industry:Challenging Times Ahead", Chartered Financial Analyst, February 2007, pp. 68-70.

E-Banking Management
Edited by: Dr. Rabi N. Misra
ISBN: 978-93-5056-788-3
Edition: 2016
Published by: Discovery Publishing House Pvt. Ltd., New Delhi (India)

Electronic Frauds in Banks
Causes and Cures

Dr. M. Trimurthi Rao
Asst. Professor
Dept. of Sociology & Social Work
Acharya Nagarjuna University
Nagarjuna Nagar, Guntur, A.P.

Introduction to E-banking transaction

An electronic banking transaction involves the transmission of an electronic message from the customer to the bank directing the bank to transfer money from his account to another account either in the same bank or to another branch or any other bank anywhere in the world. This may also be a bank's electronic communication regarding the credit or debit card statement to a customer, which essentially and mostly is a statement of account.

E-banking still does not account for a significant portion of total transactions in India as per RBI. The generation today is increasingly opting for net transactions to settle their utility bills and do all kinds of bank-related work. With increased online usage, online frauds have also increased. E-banking transactions are made safe, its integrity and authenticity preserved by encrypting the messages. These messages are further hashed and converted into a digital signature with a private key having a secret and individualistic signer. Digital signatures cannot be unwrapped or tampered. A key pair is generated by the subscriber using asymmetric crypto system and is registered with the controlling authorities. While the private key remains with the subscriber, the other key remains with the controlling authorities and is published and is available to persons who need them.

Definition of Fraud

'Fraud' can be defined as "any behaviour by which one person intends to gain a dishonest advantage over another". In other words, fraud is an act or omission which is intended to cause wrongful gain to one person and wrongful loss to the other, either by way of concealment of facts or otherwise. Electronic fraud is the use of electronic devices to fraud someone. Hackers gain access to client information like visa card numbers, social security numbers and passwords. The information is then copied to computers under the hackers control for analysis and exploitation.

Frauds in the banking sector: Some statistics

A comparative data (Table 11 of total number of fraud cases and amount involved as on March 31, 2013 for Scheduled Commercial Banks, NBFCs, Urban Co-operative Banks, and Financial Institutions is as under:

It is evident from the above Table, the cumulative number of frauds reported by the banking sector and the total amount involved in these fraud cases have a major share in the frauds reported by all entities under RBI's supervisory jurisdiction. A year-wise break up of fraud cases reported by the banking sector together with the amount involved is given in Table 7.2.

Table 1: No. of fraud cases reported by RBI regulated entities.

(No. of cases in absolute terms and amount involved in Rs. crore)

Sl. No.	Category	No. of Cases	Amount Involved
1.	Commercial Banks	169190	29910.12
2.	NBFCs	935	154.78
3.	UCBs	6345	1057.03
4.	FIs	77	279.08
	Total	**176547**	**31401.01**

Table 2: Year-wise break up of fraud cases reported by the banking sector.

(No. of cases in absolute terms and amount involved in Rs. crore)

Sl.No.	Year	No. of Cases	Total Amount
1.	2009-10	24791	2037.81
2.	2010-11	19827	3832.08
3.	2011-12	14735	4491.54
4.	2012-13	13293	8646.00
Total frauds reported as of March 2013		**169190**	**29910.12**

It may be observed that while the number of fraud cases has shown a decreasing trend from 24791 cases in 2009-10 to 13293 cases in 2012-13 *i.e.* a decline of 46.37%, the amount involved has increased substantially from ₹ 2037.81 crore to ₹ 8646.00 crore *i.e.* an increase of 324.27%. A granular analysis reveals that nearly 80% of all fraud cases involved amounts less than rupees one lakh while on an aggregated basis; the amount involved in such cases was only around 2% of the total amount involved. Similarly, the large value fraud cases involving amount of ₹ 50 crore and above, has also increased more than tenfold from 3 cases in financial year 2009-10 (involving an amount of ₹ 404.13 crore) to 45 cases in financial year 2013 (involving an amount of

₹ 5334.75 crore). Further, a bank group-wise analysis of frauds reveals that while the private sector and the foreign bank groups accounted for a majority of frauds by number (82.5%), the public sector banks (including SBI Group) accounted for nearly 83% of total amount involved in all reported frauds.

Category of Frauds

Broadly, the frauds reported by banks can be divided into three main sub-groups:

- Technology related;
- KYC related (mainly in deposit accounts);
- Advances related.

A closer examination of the reported fraud cases has revealed that around 65% of the total fraud cases reported by banks were technology related frauds (covering frauds committed through/at internet banking channel, ATMs and other alternate payment channels like credit/debit/prepaid cards) while the advances portfolio accounted for a major proportion (64%) of the total amount involved in frauds. Table 3 shows that relatively large value advances related frauds (> Rs. 1 crore) have increased both in terms of number and amount involved over the last four years.

Technology Related Frauds

Banks are increasingly nudging their customers to adopt newer service delivery platforms like mobile, internet and social media, for enhanced efficiency and cost-cutting. But while banks' customers have become tech-sawy and started using online banking services and products, evidence suggests that even fraudsters are devising newer ways of perpetrating frauds by exploiting the loopholes in technology systems and processes. Bank group-wise detail of the number of technology related fraud cases with the amount involved therein over the last 4 years is as under in Table 7.4.

Table 3: Bank Group-wise Advance Related Frauds (Rs. 1 Crore & above in value)

(No. of cases in absolute terms and amount involved in Rs. Crore)

Bank Group	2009-10		2010-11		2011-12		2012-13		Cumulative total (at end of March 2013)	
	No. of cases	Amount Involved	No. of cases	Amount Involved	No. of cases	Amount Involved	No. of cases	Amount Involved	No. of cases	Amount Involved
Nationalised Banks including SBI Group	152	736.14	201	1820.12	228	2961.45	309	6078.43	1792	14577.28
Old Private Sector Banks	16	99.10	20	289.31	14	63.31	12	49.87	149	767.75
New Private Sector Banks	10	63.38	18	234.18	12	75.68	24	67.47	363	1068.18
Sub-total	**26**	**162.48**	**38**	**523.49**	**26**	**138/98**	**36**	**117.34**	**512**	**1835.93**
Foreign Banks	4	45.26	3	33.20	19	83.51	4	16.75	456	277.05
Grand Total	**182**	**943.87**	**242**	**2376.81**	**273**	**3183.94**	**349**	**6212.51**	**2760**	**16690.26**

Table 4: Bank Group-wise Technology Related Frauds

(No. of cases in absolute terms and amount involved in Rs. Crore)

Bank Group	2009-10		2010-11		2011-12		2012-13		Cumulative total (at end of March 2013)	
	No. of cases	Amount Involved	No. of cases	Amount Involved	No. of cases	Amount Involved	No. of cases	Amount Involved	No. of cases	Amount Involved
Nationalised Banks including SBI Group	118	1.82	143	3.39	172	7.26	190	9.85	824	25.60
Old Private Sector Banks	9	0.15	4	0.46	9	0.06	6	1.09	55	2.30
New Private Sector Banks	14387	34.53	9638	21.41	6552	16.54	3408	33.97	74321	183.48
Sub-total	**14396**	**34.68**	**9642**	**21.87**	**6561**	**16.6**	**3414**	**35.06**	**75200**	**211.38**
Foreign Banks	5273	26.88	4486	14.77	3315	14.60	5161	22.45	36455	145.95
Grand Total	**19787**	**63.38**	**14271**	**40.03**	**10048**	**38.46**	**8765**	**67.36**	**111655**	**357.33**

The predominance of the new private sector banks and the foreign banks in the number of technology related frauds is intuitive as they lead the technology enabled service delivery in the Indian banking sector. From the above Table 4, evident that though the incidence of cyber frauds is extremely high, the actual amount involved is generally very low. While the amounts involved may be small from banks' perspective, these are significant from the viewpoint of individuals, who are victims of such frauds. The small value of frauds, therefore, cannot be a comfort to the banks. The banks must realize that the community that uses online banking services is a very powerful group capable of launching scathing attacks using the social media, which can irreparably tarnish the reputation of banks. It is, therefore, in banks' own interest to ensure that they are constantly on the guard and up to the challenge of providing a secure environment for customers to conduct banking transactions.

Measures to deal with Electronic frauds

(1) **Monitoring System:** The banks would need to constantly monitor the, typology of the fraudulent activities in such transactions and regularly review and update the existing security features to prevent easy manipulation by hackers, skimmers, phishers, etc. With cyber attack becoming more frequent, RBI has advised banks in February 2013 to introduce certain minimum checks and balances like introduction of two factor authentication in case of 'card not present' transactions, converting all strip based cards to chip based cards for better security, issuing debit and credit cards only for domestic usage unless sought specifically by the customer, putting threshold limit on international usage of debit/ credit cards, constant review of the pattern of card transactions in coordination with customers, sending SMS alerts in respect of card transactions etc., to minimize the impact of such attacks on banks as well as customers.

(2) **Electronic modes of payment:** The electronic modes of payment like NEFT and RTGS have gained traction due to their almost real time impact and also comparatively lower cost. These transactions are generally undertaken remotely, through internet banking, by using specific ID and password provided to the users. Though, it is the responsibility of the user to ensure that his unique ID and password are properly secured and do not get misused due to his laxity, the banks, on their part, should also ensure that these payment channels are safe and secure.

(3) **Preventive measures:** Introduction of preventive measures such as putting a cap on the value/number of beneficiaries, introducing system of issuing alert on inclusion of additional beneficiary, velocity checks on number of transactions effected per day/per beneficiary, considering introduction of digital signature for large value payments, capturing internet protocol check as an additional validation check for any transaction, etc., would prove to be beneficial in preventing frauds.

(4) **Replication of data:** Instances of frauds by way of replication of data contained in genuine debit/credit cards onto duplicate cards have become common recently. Banks need to improve the peripheral and system security in ATM locations and, at the same time, educate their customers about using their payment cards with due caution.

(5) **Fraudulent e-mails and SMS messages:** Cases of circulation of fraudulent e-mails and SMS messages conveying winning of prize money have become matter of common occurrence in recent times. Many a times, gullible people fall prey to such e-mails and pay money in designated accounts, which is then quickly siphoned off through ATMs located in far flung areas of the country. For this purpose, the fraudsters generally use deposit accounts in banks with lax KYC drills or accounts which remain inoperative for long. Banks, therefore, not only

need to caution their customers to guard against such temptations for easy money but should also ensure that deposit accounts maintained with them are fully KYC compliant. In fact, inadequacy of KYC drill would render any subsequent investigation process meaningless. The banks should also have a system of generating alerts to monitor transactions in accounts which are inoperative for long or where transactions are not in conformity with general trend and customer risk profile.

6. **Exchange of information:** Though the amount involved in technology related frauds may not appear to be menacing when viewed in the backdrop of the total value of daily transactions and overall business prolife of the Indian banks, any dent in the confidence of the stakeholders in the banking system will result in huge reputational and operational risks for the banks, adversely affect public perception and undermine faith in the financial system. If the banks are not able to proactively manage the technology risks in their delivery systems, they may have to face litigations on customer protection and also incur the wrath of the regulators and customer interest groups. Apart from enlisting active co-operation from their technology vendors, banks must look to build a close rapport with other banks, investigative agencies and regulators to ensure that there is prompt and coordinated exchange of information, whenever required.
7. **Engage with the telecom service providers:** With the spread of mobile banking, banks would also need to closely engage with the telecom service providers for reducing the technology related fraud risk. Banks could also consider seeking insurance coverage as a risk transfer tool and a mitigate for the financial losses arising from technology induced fraudulent customer transactions.
8. **Fixing of Staff Accountability:** Another area demanding urgent attention of banks is fixing of staff accountability. I believe there is a pressing need to probe staff

accountability in a fair and objective manner and take it to its logical conclusion. This is necessary to instil a sense of responsibility amongst the officials for complying with the laid down procedures.

9. Checking the credit history of the borrower: Today, most banks have put in place a system of checking the credit history of the borrower through credit information companies like the CIBIL. Considering that fraudulent borrowers could still seek credit from the banking system even after defrauding one bank, it may be worthwhile to consider setting up a fraud registry on the lines of credit information bureau. This, coupled with stringent deterrents such as prohibition of banking facilities to fraudulent borrowers, may serve as a strong antidote to the malaise.

CONCLUSION

The impact of frauds on entities like banks, which are engaged in financial activities, is more significant as their operations involve intermediation of funds. The economic cost of frauds can be huge in terms of likely disruption in the working of the markets, financial institutions, and the payment system. Besides, frauds can have a potentially debilitating effect on confidence in the banking system and may damage the integrity and stability of the economy. It can bring down banks, undermine the central bank's supervisory role and even create social unrest, discontent and political upheavals. The vulnerability of banks to fraud has been heightened by technological advancements in recent times.

The advantages of technology, communication and accessibility of data must be leveraged to put in place a system wide fraud mitigation mission. Any house is only as strong as its foundation and as weather proof as its insulation. It is necessary, therefore, that a strong foundation is built by leveraging robust IT systems, framing effective policies and procedures, laying down strict compliance processes, setting high integrity standards, developing efficient monitoring capabilities and initiating strict punitive action against the culprits in a time bound manner. It is also imperative that we insulate ourselves from unscrupulous activities by strengthening the fraud detection, mitigation and control mechanism through prompt identification, investigation and exchange of information. This is necessary not just for the safety of banks but for ensuring the stability and resilience of the overall financial system and sustaining the , confidence that various stakeholders have in its strength and integrity.

REFERENCES

Advanced Bank management, IIBF.

Banking and Finance Review, 2012.

Banking Awareness, Arihant Experts, 2012 Journal of Banking & Finance, January, 2013.

International Journal of Banking Accounting and Finance, June 2012.

Journal of Banking and Finance, January 2013.

Legal and Regulatory Aspects of Banking, IIBF (Indian Institute of Banking and Finance).

Murray N. Rothboard, The Mystery of Banking, 2011.

N.K.Sinha, Money Banking and Finance.

Naina Lal Kidwani, Contemporary Banking in India.

Principles and Practices of Banking, IIBF.

RBI Bulletin, 2012.

The Banker, 2012.

E-Banking Management
Edited by: Dr. Rabi N. Misra
ISBN: 978-93-5056-788-3
Edition: 2016
Published by: Discovery Publishing House Pvt. Ltd., New Delhi (India)

CHAPTER 8 Internet Banking in India

Dr. S.K. Badatya
Asst. Prof. in Finance
PGCMS, MBA Dept., Ankushpur, Berhampur, Ganjam Odisha

Dr. R.N. Misra
Prof. MBA, SMJT, BPUT, Ankushpur, Barhampur

Introduction

E-banking refers to Electronic Banking. It is like e-business in banking industry. It is also called as "Virtual Banking" or "Online Banking". E-banking is a result of the growing expectations of bank's customers. It involves information technology based banking. Internet banking (or E-banking) means any user with a personal computer and a browser can get connected to his banks website to perform any of the virtual banking functions. In this system the bank has a centralized database that is web-enabled. All the services that the bank has permitted on the internet are displayed in menu. Any service can be selected and further interaction is dictated by the nature of service. The traditional branch model of bank is now giving place to an alternative delivery channels with ATM network. Once the branch offices of bank are interconnected through terrestrial or satellite links, there would be no physical identity for any branch. It would a borderless entity permitting anytime, anywhere and anyhow banking. The network which connects the various locations and gives connectivity to the central office within the organization is called intranet. These networks are limited to organizations for which they are set-up. You can now get all your accounts details, submit requests and undertake a wide range of transactions online. Our E-Banking service makes banking a lot more easy and effect.

The Reserve Bank of India constituted a working group on Internet Banking. The group divided the internet banking products in India into 3 types based on the levels of access granted:

(*i*) **Information Only System:** General purpose information like interest rates, branch location, bank products and their features, loan and deposit calculations are provided in the banks website. There exist facilities for downloading various types of application forms. The communication is normally done through e-mail. There is no interaction between the customer and bank's application system. No identification of the customer is done. In this system, there is no possibility of any unauthorized person getting into production systems of the bank through internet.

(*ii*) **Electronic Information Transfer System:** The system provides customer-specific information in the form of account balances, transaction details, and statement of accounts. The information is still largely of the 'read only' format. Identification and authentication of the customer is through password. The information is fetched from the bank's application system either in batch mode or off-line. The application systems cannot directly access through the internet.

(*iii*) **Fully Electronic Transactional System:** This system allows bi-directional capabilities. Transactions can be submitted by the customer for online update. This system requires high degree of security and control. In this environment, web server and application systems are linked over secure infrastructure. It comprises technology covering computerization, networking and security, inter-bank payment gateway and legal infrastructure.

Automated Teller Machine (ATM)

ATM is designed to perform the most important function of bank. It is operated by plastic card with its special features. The plastic card is replacing cheque, personal attendance of the customer, banking hours restrictions and paper based verification. There are debit cards. ATMs used as spring board for Electronic Fund Transfer. ATM itself can provide information about customers account and also receive instructions from customers - ATM cardholders. An ATM is an Electronic Fund Transfer terminal capable of handling cash deposits, transfer between accounts, balance enquiries, cash withdrawals and pay bills. It may be on-line or Off-line. The on-line ATN enables the customer to avail banking facilities from anywhere. In off-line the facilities are confined to that particular ATM assigned. Any customer possessing ATM card issued by the Shared Payment Network System can go to any ATM linked to Shared Payment Networks and perform his transaction.

Credit Cards/Debit Cards

The Credit Card holder is empowered to spend wherever and whenever he wants with his Credit Card within the limits fixed by his bank. Credit Card is a post-paid card. Debit Card, on the other hand, is a pre-paid card with some stored value. Every time a person uses this card, the Internet Banking house gets money transferred to its account from the bank of the buyer. The buyers account is debited with the exact amount of purchases. An individual has to open an account with the issuing bank which gives debit card with a Personal Identification Number (PIN). When he makes a purchase, he enters his PIN on shops PIN pad. When the card is slurped through the electronic terminal, it dials the acquiring bank system - either Master Card or VISA that validates the PIN and finds out from the issuing bank whether to accept or decline the transactions. The customer can never overspend because the system rejects any transaction which exceeds the balance in his account. The bank never faces a default because the amount spent is debited immediately from the customer's account.

Smart Card

Banks are adding chips to their current magnetic stripe cards to enhance security and offer new service, called Smart Cards. Smart Cards allow thousands of times of information storable on magnetic stripe cards. In addition, these cards are highly secure, more reliable and perform multiple functions. They hold a large amount of personal information, from medical and health history to personal banking and personal preferences.

Services available through E-Banking

Bill Payment Service: You can facilitate payment of electricity and telephone bills, mobile phone, credit card and insurance premium bills as each bank has tie-ups with various utility companies, service providers and insurance companies, across the country. To pay your bills, all you need to do is complete a simple one-time registration for each biller. You can also set-up standing instructions online to pay your recurring bills, automatically. Generally, the bank does not charge customers for online bill payment.

Fund Transfer: You can transfer any amount from one account to another of the same or any another bank. Customers can send money anywhere in India. Once you login to your account, you need to mention the payees' account number, his bank and the branch. The transfer will take place in a day or so, whereas in a traditional method, it takes about three working days. ICICI Bank says that online bill payment service and fund transfer facility have been their most popular online services.

Credit Card Customers: With Internet banking, customers can not only pay their credit card bills online but also get a loan on their cards. If you lose your credit card, you can report lost card online.

Railway Pass: This is something that would interest all the aam janta. Indian Railways has tied up with ICICI bank and you can now make your Railway Pass for local trains online. The pass will be delivered to you at your doorstep. But the facility is limited to Mumbai, Thane, Nashik, Surat and Pune.

Investing through Internet Banking: You can now open an FD online through funds transfer. Now investors with interlinked demat account and bank account can easily trade in the stock market and the amount will be automatically debited from their respective bank accounts and the shares will be credited in their demat account. Moreover, some banks even give you the facility to purchase mutual funds directly from the online banking system. Nowadays, most leading banks offer both online banking and demat account. However if you have your demat account with independent share brokers, then you need to sign a special form, which will link your two accounts.

Recharging your Pre-paid Phone: Now just top-up your pre-paid mobile cards by logging in to Internet banking. By just selecting your operator's name, entering your mobile number and the amount for recharge, your phone is again back in action within few minutes.

Shopping: With a range of all kind of products, you can shop online and the payment is also made conveniently through your account. You can also buy railway and air tickets through Internet banking.

Advantages of the Internet Banking

1. **24*7 access to your account:** The conventional banking system will allow you to operate your personal day only on the week days and during the banking hours. However the internet banking will give you the privilege of the 24*7 operations and access to your account. You can perform all your banking related stuff from your own place and at your convenient time.
2. **Transaction made easy:** Sometime you may have to make some payment on the schedule dates else you have to pay the penalty for it. In case of the traditional banking system, you have to put a reminder for all the future transaction and payments. However in real practice it is very difficult to memories all the future transaction. The internet banking will give you the freedom from it. The system will automatically remind you for all your future transaction. In addition to that if you will opt for the standing instruction option, the system will take care of the future transaction.
3. **Settlement of transaction in no time:** The internet banking has been developed with an aim to make it user friendly and the attempt has succeeded also. If you are making any financial transaction through the internet banking, the transaction will be settled in no time and you will receive your transaction status immediately.

Disadvantages of the Internet Banking

(*i*) **Legal issue:** All the internet banking transactions are settled by the users only as well as the authorization also. In case of any financial disturbance, it requires an authentication from the banking staff. In case of the internet banking the authorization can't be obtained from the banking personal and it will invite the legal complaints.

(*ii*) **Lack of human touch:** Banking is all together a service industry. A service industry always has an upper hand, when there is a customer care with human touch. In case of the traditional banking system the banking staff will assist you in case of any difficulties. However the internet banking lacks this option. The user will not have a direct contact with the customer contact personal. Though there will be an option to talk over the phone to talk to the customer care personal, you don't have the guarantee that you are talking to the best person available there.

(*iii*) **The security aspects:** All internet banking service providers are leaving no stone unturned to make their service a fool proof one. Still there exists a threat to the internet banking. To make your internet banking account a secure one, just follow the guidelines issued by the bank and do not share your login details with anyone.

Product and Services Offered through Internet Banking Facility

Presently Internet Banking Services intends to provide following On-line & Off-line Services to our customers.

(A) ONLINE Services:

1. **Account Summary:** Accounts which are 'Internet Banking Enabled' may be displayed along with the Current Balance, Total Balance, Unclear Balance and Available Balance etc. (Savings/Current/Overdraft/Term Deposit/ Loan Accounts).
2. **Overdraft Details:** Limit and Drawing Power for OD Accounts, Repayment Schedule for Loan Accounts may be viewed.
3. **Transactions Details:** User may view, download and print of the last 14 transactions or for specified period of selected account.
4. **Online Requests:** User may request for Stop Payment for a particular Cheque or Range of Cheques in select accounts, Revoke of Stop Payment of Cheques already stopped. User may also change his contact no. (phone no., mobile no., e-mail etc.)

5. **Funds Transfer between own Accounts:** User may transfer funds from one account (with requested transaction facility) to his/her another account to the extent of fund transfer limit fixed by the bank from time to time, subject to the available balance, by selecting 'from' 'to' accounts.
6. **Adding of Account in Beneficiary List:** If amounts are frequently transferred to a particular account, then the facility of adding that account in beneficiary list will be available by providing a nick name to that account.
7. **Viewing of Beneficiary Accounts:** User may view all the beneficiaries that have been added and may also modify the details of a beneficiary by selecting that beneficiary.
8. **Fund transfer to other beneficiary Account:** User may transfer fund from his/her account (with requested transaction facility) to any other third party account, maintained with any of our CBS Branch, to the extent of fund transfer limit fixed by the bank from time to time, subject to the available balance, by selecting his/her account and giving either third party's account number or selecting a beneficiary.
9. **Standing Order:** User may give standing order for transfer of funds from one account to another to be executed on a predefined frequency (daily /monthly / month end). User may also amend or cancel the standing order so given.
10. **E-Payment Facilities:** User may use E-Payment facility for payment of Direct (CBDT) and Indirect (CBEC) taxes by debiting the account online and may print cyber receipt and challan also.

Online Enquiry

(*i*) **Cheque Enquiry:** User may enquire status of a Cheque or Range of Cheques issued in an account.

(*ii*) **Cheque Books:** User may enquire for Cheque Books issued in an account.

(*iii*) **Outward Cheques Enquiry:** User may enquire status of specific Cheque or all Cheques deposited in an account.

(*iv*) **TDS Detail:** User may view the Tax Deducted at Source details.

Other Options

(*i*) **Contact Details:** User may view address details.

(*ii*) **Change Login Password:** User may change login password as per guidelines available on website.

(*iii*) **Change Transaction Password:** User may change transaction password as per guidelines available on website.

(*iv*) **Change User Preference:** User can change their User-Id; however the same can be changed.

(*v*) **Only Once:** User may set his/her display preference.

(*vi*) **Login History:** User may view login history.

(B) Off-line Services

1. **Deposit Account Opening:** User may request for opening of deposit account by selecting the account from which the amount is to be debited and giving the deposit details.
2. **Deposit Amend/Renewal:** User may request for amendment of deposit account (only Interest repayment mode, and Maturity Instruction).
3. **Closure of Deposit Account:** User may request for closure of deposit account by giving the repayment details.
4. **Issuance of Demand Drafts and Delivery Options:** User may request for issue of Demand Draft by giving the details of draft and delivery options.
5. **Account Statement:** User may request for account statement by selecting account, period of statement and delivery options.
6. **Cheque Book Issue:** User may request for issue of Cheque Book in selected account and delivery option.
7. **Funds Transfer Facility:** User may request for Funds Transfer Facility (Transaction) in an account by selecting account.

8. **Account Transfer:** User may request for transfer of account from one branch to another branch (the types of account eligible for transfer may be decided by Bank).
9. **Phone Banking:** User may request for Phone Banking Facility by giving one default account.
10. **SMS Banking:** User may request for SMS Banking Facility by giving one default account.
11. **Loan Account Opening:** User may request for a Loan by giving details of loan type, amount, period, annual income etc.
12. **Request Status Enquiry:** User may view the status of a request already submitted by giving request Id or date range or request status. The present status of the request is displayed (Processed/Pending/Rejected).
13. **Modeling:** Viewing of EMI: User may view the EMI for selected Loan Product for a given amount and loan period.
14. **Deposit Modeling:** User may view the maturity amount for selected Deposit Product for a given amount and deposit period.

The Future Scenario of Internet Banking

Compared to banks abroad, Indian banks offering online services still have a long way to go. For online banking to reach a critical mass, there has to be sufficient number of users and the sufficient infrastructure in place. WAP (Wireless Application Protocol) telephony is the merger of mobile telephony with the Internet. It offers two-way connectivity, unlike Mobile Banking where the customer communicates to a mailbox answering machine. WAP may provide the infrastructure for P2P (person to person) or P2M (person to merchant) payment. In addition to customers' deposit accounts, they also maintain demat accounts of their clients. Online trading in equities is being allowed by SEBI. This is another area which banks are keen to get into. Internet banking thus promises to become a popular delivery channel not only for retail banking products but also for online securities trading. Reserve Bank of India has taken the initiative for facilitating real time funds transfer through the Real Time Gross Settlement (RTGS) System. Under the RTGS system, transmission, processing and settlements of the instructions will be done on a continuous basis. Gross settlement in a real time mode eliminates credit and liquidity risks.

REFERENCES

Ch. Satyanarayana, and S. Sirisha., "An Overview of Automated Teller Machine (ATMs)", Dharohar, IJM, Vol. 1, Issues.2, Dec. 2012, P. 1-6.

Chandrasekhar, C.P, "How Sound is Indian Banking ", Economic and Political Weekly, Vol. XLIV, No. 19, May'9-15, 2009, P. 08.

Dheenadhayalan, V., "Automation of Banking Sector in India", Yojana, Vol. 54, Feb.10, P. 32.

Kumar, Akhilesh., Service Sector: Can it be the engine of Inclusive Growth", Yojana. 2011, Vol. 55, P.17.

Maheswari, S.N., and Maheswari, S.K. Banking Law & Practice. New Delhi. Kalyani Publisher, 2009.

Narsis, I "Banking Service Quality and its Impact on Customer Satisfaction", The Economic Challenger, No.-II, Issue-41, Oct.-Dec.' 2009. P. 47-50.

Saravanam, M. and Chandrasekhran, B., "Growth trends in Service Sector", Yojana. Sept. 2011, Vol. 55, P.13.

E-Banking Management
Edited by: Dr. Rabi N. Misra
ISBN: 978-93-5056-788-3
Edition: 2016
Published by: Discovery Publishing House Pvt. Ltd., New Delhi (India)

E-Banking in Indian Commercial Banks

Dr. S. Vijayulu Reddy
Reader in Commerce,
Visvodaya Government Degree, College,
Venkatagiri

Introduction

There has been a paradigm shift in the Indian banking industry in the way they operate and manage their diversified banking portfolio especially during the last one decade. More and more new products and services are now being handled by banks on technology platform. Technology is acting as a catalyst and an enabler for bringing in speed, efficiency and accuracy in handling the complex banking functions and ever-changing needs of the customers. With the major initiatives undertaken by the Reserve Bank of India (RBI) and Institute for Development and Research in Banking Technology (IDRBT), banks have achieved considerable level of infusion of contemporary technology in their operations.

Technological Advance in Banking

With competition as the buzzword among banks, all categories of banks have been investing on computerization and use of advanced communication networks. The directive by Central Vigilance Commission (CVC) to banks to achieve 100 per cent computerization has imparted urgency to the process of technological advancement. While new private sector banks, foreign banks and a few older private sector banks have been enjoying a head start in adopting "Core Banking Solutions", "Public Sector Banks (PSBs)" too have fallen in line rather vigorously. The application of information technology in banking sector resulted in the development of different concepts of banking sector such as E-banking.

Internet-banking, Online Banking, Telephone Banking, Automated Teller Machine, Universal Banking and Investment Banking etc., with quick electronic services to the dynamic customers of information society.

Different Banks are in different stages of implementation of Electronic Banking. There is no denying the fact that foreign banks and new generation private sector banks are forerunners in this area of implementation of Electronic Banking solutions. Citibank, HDFC bank and ICICI bank have already started their e-commerce portals. These banks are already offering on-line real time banking services on Internet. The new private sector banks and foreign banks could implement the Electronic Banking solutions comparatively faster because of their smaller network of branches and these banks already have a centralized database which could easily be linked with the world-wide-web to offer e-commerce and e-banking facility. The PSBs are also competing with private sector banks but still they are lagging behind due to large volume of clientele and rural branches.

Developments in Banking Sector

- **Society for Worldwide Inter-bank Financial Tele-communications (SWIFT):** SWIFT, as a co-operative society was formed in May 1973 with 239 participating banks from 15 countries with RS headquarters at Brussels. It started functioning in May 1977. Reserve Bank of India and other public sector banks as well as 8 foreign banks in India have obtained the membership of the SWIFT. SWIFT provides rapid, secure, reliable and cost effective mode of transmitting the financial messages worldwide.

- **Automated Teller Machine (ATM) :** ATM is an electronic machine, which is operated by the customer himself to make deposits, withdrawals and other financial transactions. ATM is a step in improvement in customer service. ATM facility is available to the customer 24 hours a day.

  The customer is issued an ATM card. This is a plastic card, which bears the customer's name. This card is magnetically coded and can be read by this machine. Each cardholder is provided with a secret Personal Identification Number (PIN). When the customer wants to use the card, he has to insert his plastic card in the slot of the machine. After the card is recognized by the machine, the customer enters his personal identification number. After establishing the authentication of the customers, the ATM allows the customer to enter the amount to be withdrawn by him. After processing that transaction and finding sufficient balances in his account, the output slot of ATM give the required cash to him. When the transaction is completed, the ATM ejects the customer's card.

- **Electronic Clearing Service:** In 1994, RBI appointed a committee to review the mechanization in the banks and also to review the electronic clearing service. The committee recommended in its report that electronic clearing service-credit clearing facility should be made available to all corporate bodies/Government institutions for making repetitive low value payment like dividend, interest, refund, salary, pension or commission, it was also recommended by the committee Electronic Clearing Service - Debit clearing may be introduced for pre-authorized debits for payments of utility bills, insurance premium and installments to leasing and financing companies. RBI has been necessary step to introduce these schemes, initially in Chennai, Mumbai, Calcutta and New Delhi.

- **Banknet:** Banknet a first national level network in India, which was commissioned in February 1991. It is communication network established by RBI on the basis of recommendation of the Committee appointed by it under the Chairmanship of the Executive Director T.NA. Lyre. Banknet has two phases : Banknet-1 and Banknet-II.

Areas of Operation and Application of Banknet

- The message of banking transaction can be transferred in the form of codes from the city to the other.
- Quick settlement of transactions and advices.
- Improvement in customer service—withdrawal of funds is possible from any member branch,
- Easy transfer of data and other statements to RBI.
- Useful in foreign exchange dealings.
- Access to SWIFT through Banknet is easily possible.
- **Phone Banking:** Customers can now dial up the bank's designed telephone number and he by dialing his ID number will be able to get connectivity to bank's designated computer. The software provided in the machine interactive with the computer asking him to dial the code number of the service required by him and suitably answers him. By using Automatic Voice Recorder (AVR) for simple quarries and transactions and manned phone terminals for completed queries and transactions, the customer can actually do entire non-cash relating banking on telephone: Anywhere, Anytime.
- **Tele-banking:** Tele-banking is another innovation, which provided the facility of 24 hour banking to the customer. Tele-banking is based on the voice processing facility available on bank computers. The caller usually a customer calls the bank anytime and can enquire balance in his account or other transaction history. In this system, the computers at bank are connected to a telephone link

with the help of a modem. Voice processing facility is provided in the software. This software identifies the voice of caller and provides him suitable reply. Some banks also use telephonic answering machine but this is limited to some brief functions. This is only telephone answering system and now tele-banking. Tele-banking is becoming popular since queries at ATM's are now becoming too long.

- **Internet Banking :** Internet banking enables a customer to do banking transactions through the bank's website on the Internet. It is a system of accessing accounts and general information on bank products and services through a computer while sitting in his office or home. This is also called virtual banking. It is more or less bringing the bank to your computer. In traditional banking one has to approach the branch in person, to withdraw cash or deposit a cheque or request a statement of accounts etc., but Internet banking has changed the way of computer through website of bank. All such transactions are encrypted; using sophisticated multi-layered security architecture, including firewalls and filters. One can be rest assured that one's; transactions are secure and confidential.
- **Mobile Banking :** Mobile banking facility is an extension of internet banking. The bank is association with the cellular service providers offers this service. For this service, mobile phone should either be SMS or WAP enabled. These facilities are available even to those customers with only credit card accounts with the bank.
- **Anywhere Banking :** With expansion of technology, it is now possible to obtain financial details from the bank from remote locations. Basic transaction can be effected from far-a-way places. Automated Teller Machines are playing an important role in providing remote services to the customers. Withdrawals from other stations have been possible due to inter-station connectivity of ATM's. The

Rangarajan Committee had also suggested the installation of ATM at non-branch locations, airports, hotels, railway stations etc., remote banking is being further extended to the customer's office and home.

- **Voice Mail :** Talking of answering systems, there are several banks mainly foreign banks now offering very advanced touch tone telephone answering service which route the customer call directly to the department concerned and allow the customer to leave a message for the concerned desk or department, if the person is not available.
- **Core Banking Solutions:** Most of the banks in India have implemented technology solutions and are at different stages of implementation of the Core Banking Solutions (CBS). As we all know CBS is a transactions handling platform, created to ensure quick and easy implementation of a cross-section of innovative products and services for different strata of customer segments. Centralized database in CBS environment enables the banks to offer whole host of services to their customers along various delivery channels.

Implications of E-Commerce for Banks in India

Banks in India stand to benefit immensely by implementing banking-related E-Commerce applications. Just to use one yardstick, the customer base in Internet banking offered by Indian banks to their customers, has increased dramatically. This augurs well in terms of business possibilities of bank in India. Some of the specific implications in implementing E-Commerce solutions by banks in India, are as follows :

- Two major developments in the area of technology namely, computerization and networking have impacted banking operations in our country. As a consequence of these developments, there are new avenues of diversifying and augmenting revenues from banking business. Internet banking is a major thrust area.

- The induction of the Electronic Clearing System (ECS), Automated Teller Machines (ATMs), Cash Dispensers and Credit/Debit Cards has truly made banking customer-focused. Moreover, Electronic Funds Transfer (EFT), Home Banking, Smart Cards and Internet Banking will result in the formation of a culture of Electronic Banking in India.
- The Indian banking industry is gearing itself for "Anywhere/ Anytime Banking" which is making banking business distance-independent and seamless. The concept of banking is also undergoing a broad-based shift from "Total Branch Automation" to "Total Bank Automation". Many banks in India have introduced home/telephone banking. Internet based banking has also been introduced by some banks in India for attracting customers globally.
- The satellite-based communication network Indian Financial Network (INFINET) is expected to speed up transmission of information in the Indian banking industry.

An important thrust area in the financial sector relates to the design and development of a sophisticated payment and settlement system in conformity with global standards. This requires the setting up of an efficient and risk free Real Time Gross Settlement (RTGS) system that is in tune with the rest of the world. The experience that is gained by banks in India in developing and implementing banking-related E-Commerce applications and solutions would contribute immensely to the ongoing efforts for designing a sophisticated and risk free Payment and Settlement System.

E-Commerce in India is at a nascent stage but will grow quickly on account of the positive and encouraging developments that are taking place in the industry, such as framing of a comprehensive cyber-law, setting up of a national digital certification authority, providing global level telecom infrastructure with competitive tariffs and permitting private Internet Service Providers to set up gateways. Slowly but surely, E-Commerce is making the banking industry seamless. Banks in India can reap the benefits of participation in E-Commerce.

E-Banking Management
Edited by: Dr. Rabi N. Misra
ISBN: 978-93-5056-788-3
Edition: 2016
Published by: Discovery Publishing House Pvt. Ltd., New Delhi (India)

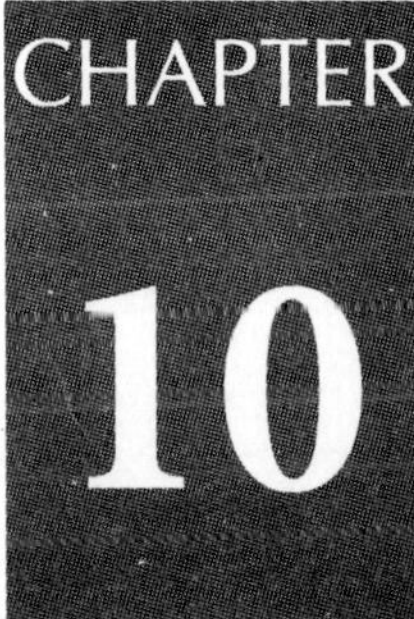

Challenges of the E-Banking Revolution

Gayatri Mandal
Asst. Prof. PG Centre for Management Studies, BPUT, SMIT, Ankushpur, Berhampur, Odisha
Dr. R.N. Misra
Prof. MBA, PGCMS, SMIT, BPUT

Introduction

Today's world is one with increasing on line access to service. E-banking in e-business in banking industry, it is an electronic payment system that enables customer of a financial institution to conduct financial transaction on a website operated by the institution, such as a retail bank, virtual bank. It is also referred as internet banking, online banking, and virtual banking. The internet has become a major platform for all financial, banking and commercial transaction in the present secenario. ATM are at our doorstep. Banking services are accessible 24 × 7 as Information Technology has become a necessary tool in today organization.

This study focuses on e-banking and its challenges in present as well as future scenario.

Evolution of E-Banking

E-banking came into being in UK and USA in 1920. It became popular during 1960 through electronic fund transfer and credit card. Web based banking came into existence in Europe and USA in 1980.

Popular Services Covered under E-Banking

- A Automated Teller Machine;
- Credit Card;
- Debit Card;
- Smart Card;
- Electronic Fund Transfer (EFT) System;
- Cheques Truncation Payment System;
- Mobile Banking Internet Banking;
- Telephone Banking.

E-BANKING IN INDIA

The traditional model for banking has been through branch banking. In India Internet Banking started in early 1990s. ICICI Bank was the first to launch internet banking in India followed by Citibank and HDFC Bank. The IT Act, 2000 was enacted by the Government of India in 2000 with effect from October 17, 2000. The RBI is monitoring and reviewing the legal and other requirement of e-banking on a continuous basis.

Advantage of Internet Banking Facility

The internet has afforded open access to customer in global market place. The Six primary drivers of Internet Banking includes:

- Improve customer access.
- Facilitates the offering of more services.
- Increase customer loyalty.
- Attract new customer.
- Provide services offered by competitors.
- Reduce customer attrition.

Advantages of E-Banking over Physical Bank Branch

E-Banking makes our day more flexible convenience:

- It saves time and money by deeding with day to day banking business.
- NO Q—By banking online we don't have to wait in line to get our banking done.
- Availability—With on line banking we can keep track of our money much easier because our account information is available any time online.
- Innovation—Checking our balance by SMS or receive alert when money is withdrawn or check clears are some information we get from our cell phone. Thus in many way online banking provides a better experience than a physical bank branch.

Banking on Internet and Mobile is Gaining Popularity

A research firm estimated that 110 million people worldwide used mobile banking and related services in 2010.

Lower cost of connectivity,. Greater internet and mobile Internet penetration, arrival of smart phone have made E-banking popular around the world.

Security Threats

Despite advancement in security technology fraudstero still manage to breach banks defenses from time to time phishing, pharmint, hacking, key stroke logging have become the modes of attack. Around 18000 phising attack takes place every month around the world. 3% of internet users from the EU27 group of countries lost money to online fraud last year.

Idea third most affected nation by online banking malware after Japan and US.

Authentication Mechanism for Customer

At present authentication of online banking user is done using user ID and password, users may be required to ensure that their password are string. Finger print, retinal image and voice are some other authenticated models.

Challenges in E-Banking

1. Lack of regulatory framework trust security and privacy standard customer investor protections hinder progress in implementing e-banking in a large scale.
2. An adequate level of infrastructure and human capacity building are required for global technology or to process e-payment
3. The co-operative effort between the private and public sectors in essential to facilitate public support for e-finance.

Problem in E-Banking

- Lack of proper integration of related system.
- Non-web enabled business process.
- Lack of understand customer communication.
- Limited Research development.
- Lack of E-commerce promotion within the organization.
- A customer may have to face some risky transaction of fraud.
- Failure or interruptions of power supply cause to break down in E-banking.

FUTURE E-BANKING IN INDIA

Banking in India has rapidly innovated to keep up with the times. Banks today are competing with each other offering low rate on having loan, credit card, etc.

Changes Ahead

The contours of the banking industry in India is set to change in the coming years with parliament passing the much awaited Banking Laws Amendment Bill.

70% of the market lies with the public sector banks but the government is encouraging to open the sector to private banks. Business houses such as Aditya Birla Goup, the Tatas and Reliance have taken keen interest in entering the banking space. The Government under late Prime Minister Indira Gandhi nationalized 14 commercial banks in 1969. In 1980 6 more commercial banks were nationalized. In 1993 the Government merged New Bank of India with Punjab National Bank. In 1990, on policy of liberalization, providing licenses to several private banks came to be known as new generation banks.

Future Scenario

Indian banks offering on the services strictly have a long way to go. Though various security option like live encryption, branch connection encryptions, fire walls, digital certificates, automatic signoffs, random pop ups and disaster recovering sites are in place there is no certification Authority in India offering public key infrastructure which is absolutely necessary for online banking.

The Internet is in the public domain where by geographical boundaries are removed. Cyber crimes are difficult to be identified and controlled. To promote Internet Banking services it is necessary that the proper legal infrastructure is in place. Introduction of the Information Technology Bill by the Government in 2000 costs an obligations of confidentiality against disclosure of any electronic record register, correspondence and information except, for certain purpose and violations of the portions is a criminal offence. The Department of Telecommunication (DOT) is moving fast to make available additional bandwidth with the result that internet access will become faster in future. Banks are then moving in for technological upgradation on a large scale. Thus E-banking is expected to get a boost from such development. Reserve Bank of India (RBI) has taken the initiative for facilitating real time funds transfer through Real Time Gross Settlement (RTGS) SYSTEM. Under the transmission, processing and settlement of the instructions will be done on a continuous basis Gross settlement in a real time mode eliminates credit and liquidity risks. Following a reference made this year in Monetary and Credit Policy of the Governor, banks have been advised to develop domestic generic modal in their computerization plans to ensure seamless integration.

With the process of dematerialization of shares having gained considerable ground in recent years banks have assumed the role of depository participants. Online trading in equities is allowed by SEBI by which banks are keen to get into. HDFC Bank Ltd., has lied up with about 25 equity brokerage for enabling third party transfer of funds and securities through its business to business (B2B) portal, 'e-Net'. Demat account holders with the bank can receive securities directly from the brokers accounts. The bank has extended its web interface to the software vendors of National Stock Exchange through a tie up with NSE.IT- the InfoTech arm of the exchange. The bank functions are the payment bank for enabling fund transfer.

CONCLUSION

E-Banking is a generic term from delivery of banking service and product through electronic character such as telephone, internet, cell phone etc., it facilitates an effective payment and accounting system enhancing the speed of delivery of banking services several initiation taken by the Government of India as well on RBI has facilitate the development of E-banking in India. The Government of India enacted the IT act, 2000 which provide legal recognition to electronic transaction and other mean of electronic commerce. It used guideline on risk and control in computer and telecommunication system to all bank, advising then to evaluate the risk in the system. Internet banking has definitely made the life easy for users by providing on line access to various banking service.

REFERENCE

E.Gordon, Dr. K.Natarajan, Financial Market Services (Himalaya Publishing House)

ISBN 0-471-29219-2 Page 41 from Banking and Finance on Interent. www. hindustantimes.

Modern Banking of India by O.P. Agarwal cron, Marry J (1997) Banking and finance on the Interent, John wilay and sons.

Ogilivie, M. Bank and Customer Law in Canada (Toronto: Irurie Law, 2007)

Riturik Mukharjee, SBI launches green policy for paperless banking, financial chronicla, 27th August, 2010.

Websites of various Banks.

E-Banking Management
Edited by: Dr. Rabi N. Misra
ISBN: 978-93-5056-788-3
Edition: 2016
Published by: Discovery Publishing House Pvt. Ltd., New Delhi (India)

CHAPTER 11

Opportunities and Challenges of E-Banking in India

Mrs. Manju Prava Das
Principal
P.G. Dept. of Rural Management
S.M.I.T., Ankushpur

Introduction

Banking is the core system of any economy. In the past, the traditional-manual banking system was prevalent everywhere in India. But today, in the era of liberalization, privatization and globalization, it is difficult to think of anything without the application of Information Technology. The competition among the banks has led to the increasing total banking automation in the Indian banking industry. The e-banking system was first adopted by Finland. The rigorous use of IT in the Indian banking sector has started immediately after the recommendations of the Committee on Financial System (Narasimham Committee, 1991) were implemented in 1991. By offering world class quality services, these banks started snatching customers from Public Sector banks and they felt the heat and realized that if they do not follow the path of these banks, they would be thrown out from the banking scene within no time.

Online banking services provided by banks are as follows:

(*a*) Core Banking Solution (CBS).

(*b*) Automated Teller Machine (ATM).

(*c*) Electronic Fund Transfer (EFT).

(*d*) Real Time Gross Settlement System (RTGS).

(*e*) National Electronic Fund Transfer (NEFT).

(*f*) Mobile Banking (M-Banking).

(*g*) Smart Cards (SCS).

Core Banking: Core Banking is a general term used to describe services provided by a group of networked bank branches.

ATM (Automated Teller Machine): ATM is a Computerized machine that permits bank customers to gain access to their Accounts with Magnetically encoded plastic card and a Code number. It enables the customer to perform several banking operations without the help of Teller such as to Withdraw Cash, Make Deposits, Pay Bills, Obtain Bank Statements and Effective Cash Transfer.

Electronic Fund Transfer (EFT): EFT is another E-Banking Product facilitating Transfer of Funds from any Branch of a Bank to any other Branch of any Bank in Shorter Time. Before EFT's, intercity transfer of Money for the Customer was made through Demand Drafts, Mail Transfers and Telegraphic Transfers.

Real Time Gross Settlement System (RTGS) - It provides for an electronic based Settlement of inter Bank & Customer based transactions, with Intraday Collateralized liquidity support from RBI to the participants of the system.

National Electronic Fund Transfer (EFT) - EFT is another E-Banking Product facilitating Transfer of Funds from any Branch of a Bank to any other Branch of any Bank in Shorter

Time. Before EFT's, inter-city transfer of Money for the Customer was made through Demand Drafts, Mail Transfers and Telegraphic Transfers.

Mobile Banking: Mobile Banking is an extension of application such as Phone Banking and Online Banking. It can be defined as a channel where by Customers interact with a Bank through a Mobile Device, *e.g.* Cell Phone.

Smart Cards: Smart Cards have gained greater acceptance and Momentum as a Medium Financial Transaction. Credit Card provides Cash Free and anywhere and anytime Shopping to the Customers but with fixed limit prescribed by Banks. Debit Card, unlike Post-paid Credit Card, is a Pre-paid Card with some Stored value.

Opportunities of E-Banking

Opportunities for Customers

General banking customers have been significantly affected by the advent of e-bariking revolution:

(*a*) A banking customer's account is extremely accessible with an online account.

(*b*) Through internet banking customer can operate his account remotely from his office or home. The need for going to bank in person for every single banking activity is dispensed with.

(*c*) Internet banking lends an added advantage towards payment of utility bills. It eliminates the need to stand in long queues for the purpose of bill payment.

(*d*) All services that are usually available from the local bank can be found on a single website.

(*e*) Sharp growth in credit card/debit card usage can be majorly attributed to e-banking. A customer can shop globally without any need for carrying paper currency with him.

(*f*) By the medium of e-banking (including internet banking), banks are available 24 × 7 and are just a mouse click away.

Opportunities for Banking Sector

In addition to banking customers, growth of e-banking infrastructure in general and online banking in particular has proved to be extremely beneficial to banks and overall bank organizations on account of following:

(*a*) The concept of online banking has immensely helped the banks in putting a tab over their specific overheads and operating cost.

(*b*) The rise of internet banking has made the banks more competitive. It resulted in opening of better prospects and avenues for banking operations.

(*c*) The online banking has ensured transparency of transactions and facilitated towards removing the documentation requirements to a major extent, since majority of records under an e-banking set-up are maintained electronically.

(*d*) The reach and delivery capabilities of internet-enabled banks, proves to be significantly better than the network of physical bank branches.

Major Challenges towards E-Banking System in India

E-banking in India is in its earliest stage of development. Most of them are basic services only the deregulation of e-banking industry coupled with the emergence of new banking technology is enabling new competitors to enter the financial services markets quickly and efficiently. However it needs to be recognized that perception norms and an improvement in functioning of e-bank.

Customer Acceptance

Proper understanding of the customer is the primary aspect of the E-banking. It is known that computer literacy in India is still very low and is barrier in fast acceptance of internet. Mindset of the Indian customer heeds to be changed by giving awareness about technical terms in e-banking. Even though it adopts in the fast changing technical scenario, the obsolesce of technology fast. Hence there is always shortage of skilled personal and fear of technology puts the customer away from electric delivery channels.

Cost of Technology

In connection with Start-up cost e-banking is huge at initial level for acquiring personal computer and other equipments; oneself to do online banking is still not with reach of the middle class and upper middle class customers. The cost of maintenance of all equipments like, modem, routers, bridges and network management systems. The cost of sophisticated hardware and software and skill level of employees needed. In e-banking there is need of skilled employees or knowledgeable professionals to route the banking transaction's through the internet. Banks can employ software application developers, database administrators and training to existing bank staff on the changing systems and procedures who can handle e-banking applications under proper supervision.

Security

In a paper less transactions, many problems of security are involved. A secrecy threat as circumstensive decision to cause the economic hardship to data, destruction of network resources disclosure, modification of data or fraud, denial in services and distortion of information. Providing appropriate security of using encryption techniques, implementation of firewalls and virus protection software etc.

Legal Issues

In today's bank world, legal framework for recognizing the validity of banking transactions. Conducted through the NET is still being put in place? Information technology act provides security and legal framework for e-commerce transactions. Information technology act or RBI suggested that criterion of Digital Signature Certification Board for authentication of electric records and communication with digital signatures.

Restricted Business

Not all transactions can be carried electronically; many deposits and some withdrawals require the use of physical services. Some banks have automated to their customers (front end) but still largely depend upon manual process (back end). It result, most of clientele or customers were restricted by lack and awareness and due to technical problems.

Transparency in Offering Services

Banks will strive to adopt best practices in corporate governance and Corporate Social Responsibility {CSR) this will enhance image and can help them to enhance their confidence of international investors. Banks much towards better corporate governance standards and adoption of uniform accounting standards and disclosure requirements Adopt Proper Organization Structure: Banks may required to adopt Hatter organization structure for judicious blending of needs foe greater delegation of power, decentralization, customer centric business models, quickly reaction of customer needs, learn continuously from customers, provide customer access, whatever and however they want to transact and interact especially for catering younger IT survey population.

Untapped Rural Markets

Contributing to 70% of the total population in India is a largely untapped market for banking sector. In all urban areas banking services entered but only few big villages have the banks entered. So that the banks must reach in remaining all villages because majority of Indian still living in rural areas.

Handling Technology

Developing or acquiring the right technology, deploying it optimally and then leveraging it to the maximum extent is essential to achieve and maintain high service and efficiency standards while remaining cost effective and delivering sustainable return to shareholders. Early adopters of technology acquire significant competitive advances. Managing technology is therefore, a key challenge for the Indian banking sector.

Other Challenges

(*a*) Coping with regulatory reforms.

(*b*) Development of skill of bank personnel.

(*c*) Customer awareness and satisfaction.

(*d*) Corporate governance.

(*e*) Changing needs of customers.

(*f*) Keeping space with technology upgradation.

(*g*) Lack of common technology standards for mobile banking.

(*h*) Sustaining healthy bottom lines and increasing shareholders value.

(*i*) Structural changes.

(*j*) Man power planning.

In the past few years, the Indian banking sector has completely transformed. The banks are facing many challenges and many opportunities are available with the banks. Many financial innovations like ATMs, credit cards, RTGS, debit cards, mobile banking etc., have completely changed the face of Indian banking. But still there is a need to have more innovative solutions so that the challenges can be solved and opportunities can be availed efficiently by the banks.

REFERENCES

Chavan, J. (June 2013). Internet Bankingn—Benefits and Challenges in An Emerging Economy. International Journal of Research in Business, © Impact Journal.

E-banking in India: Progress and Prospects. Lambert Academic Publishing.

Kaptan, S.S., Choubey, N.S. (2003). Indian banking in electronic era. Sarup and Sons. New Delhi.

Karamjit Kaur and Rajneesh Singh, K. (2012). International Journal of Management and Commerce Innovations (Online). Vol. 2, Issue 1, pp: (86-93), Month: April 2014 - September 2014.

Ms. Megha Arunkumar Jain , A Study on Emerging Opportunities & Challenges Towards E-Banking System in India, IJSR, Volume : 3, Issue : 9, September 2014.

Pallab Sikdar, M. M. (2013). Internet Banking In India - A Perspective on Benefits and Challenges Involved. International Journal of Engineering, Business and Enterprise Applications (IJEBEA), 15-19.

Sathiye, M. (1999). Adoption of Internet Banking by Australian Customers: An empirical investigation. International Journal of Bank Marketing, 17(07), 101-122.

Trivedi, M.H., Patel, V.B. (2013). Problems face by customers while using e-banking facilities in India. International Journal of Scientific Research, 2(3), 121-123.

E-Banking Management
Edited by: Dr. Rabi N. Misra
ISBN: 978-93-5056-788-3
Edition: 2016
Published by: Discovery Publishing House Pvt. Ltd., New Delhi (India)

Mobile Banking, Internet Banking

Dr. R.N. Misra
Prof. MBA, PGCMS, SMIT, BPUT

K. Venu Gopal
Lecturer in Commerce,
K.R.K. Government Degree & PG College
Addanki-523201

Introduction

Development is a continuous process. Technological, innovations and improvements speed up the process of development in any sector, as banking sector has no exception in this regard. The core capital of banking is obliviously formed through the deposits received from their expected customers. Based on these volumes only they make business to earn profits. To have dearest customers they bank has to provide maximum hassle free procedures to deal various transactions. For this purpose the banking sector has also undertaken various 'research and development' activities to entertain smooth functioning of its day-to-day business. The result of this thrust, are 'mobile banking' and 'internet banking'.

Review of Literature

- SANJAY KUMAR DHANWANI, Assistant Professor, Government Degree College, Sanawal, Balrampur (C.G.),

India, in his work of 'RECENT TREND IN INDIAN BANKING SERCTOR' identified that, the banking today is re-defined and re-engineered with the use of Information Technology and it is sure that the future of banking will offer more sophisticated services to the customers with the continuous product and process innovations. Thus, there is a paradigm shift from the seller's market to buyer's market in the industry and finally it affected at the bankers level to change their approach from "conventional banking to convenience banking" and "mass banking to class banking". The shift has also increased the degree of accessibility of a common man.

- ANDREW MUSIIME & MALINGA RAMADHAN in their work on the topic of "INGTERNET BANKING, CONSUMER ADOPTION AND CUSTOMER SATISFACTION" identified that, the bank should not be complacent; instead it should be creative and innovative creating new products or services and marketing strategies that can stimulate the demand to use Internet banking services. Even if the new strategy is implemented generally, it should mainly emphasize its efforts on targeting individual clients. Internet banking service providers ought to look out for indicators of innovative ways of creating awareness about the service through participation in trade organizations, exhibitions as well as adoption of new technologies of Internet banking.
- INFOGILE TECHNOLOGIES in their article on the title of "MOBILE BANKING THE FUTURE" has expressed that the - Mobile banking has the potential to do to the mobile phone what E-mail did to the Internet Mobile Application based banking is poised to be a big m-commerce feature, and if South Korea's foray into mass mobile banking is any indication, mobile banking could well be the driving factor to increase sales of high-end mobile phones. Nevertheless, Bank's need to take a hard and deep look into the mobile usage patterns among their target customers and enable their mobile services on a technology with reaches out to

the majority of their customers and enable their mobile services on a technology with reaches out to the majority of their customers.

Research Methodoly

The data collected and compiled for this research paper is collected entirely from Secondary Sources like articles published in various books, journals and business magazines.

Objectives of the Research Paper

The Primary objective of this research paper is to identify the extent of usage, growth and advantages of mobile and internet banking. This paper is also aimed to find out the difficulties in accessing these services by the customers.

Defination of the Concept

Internet banking is where a customer can access his or her bank account via the Internet using personal computer (PC) or mobile phone and web-browser. This service enables their customers to access and perform financial transactions on their bank accounts from their web-enabled computers with Internet connection to banks' web sites any time they wish.

Discussion

Advancement in technology and its adoption improves the performance of every sector, as banking has no exceptions. The performance of banking sector by imbibing latest developments in its working patterns, like computerization, internet, has enhanced a lot from what it had in past 10 years. Now-a-days, usage of computers has been increasing almost all in all areas, irrespective whether for business or for personal.

The earliest mobile banking services were offered over SMS, a service known as SMS banking. With the introduction of *smart phones* with *WAP* support enabling the use of the *mobile web* in 1999, the first European banks started to offer mobile banking on this platform to their customers. The facility of 'Inter-net' is also made easy and convenient for all sectors.

Usage of 'mobile' phones also has been increasing equaling to the population growth rate. Under these circumstances the 'banking' sector has been improving all its rigid services by adopting the above said technology. The 'ultimate faith' of the consumer is the prime investment to the banking business. After achieving enormous success by introducing computers in their house-keeping operations, the banking sector now have been concentrating on improving their customer needs with the help of technical advancements of 'inter-net' and 'mobile' services.

Keeping the sensitiveness of technology the Reserve Bank of India has also issued many guidelines to the commercial banks in adopting the above said issues. Nevertheless these technical services in banking activity have improved a lot, up to the satisfaction of customer till to this date. Earlier for the sake various cash needs the customer has to travel from distant areas and has to fulfill many documental procedures within a time-bond frame. Even after, the customer many not satisfied with the traditional techniques. The advents of computers enable the bank to reach their customer at far-a-way places and round the clock.

Some of the ADVANTAGES by adopting 'mobile-banking' and 'internet banking' either by banker or customer has been identified below:

1. Round the clock facility is available to the customer.
2. Paper free work is entertained in housekeeping operations of bank
3. Hustle free work is experienced by the customer.
4. High level security has been provided by the bank to their customers, in dealing 'cash transactions'.
5. 'Cash recovery' service is also possible in case of 'mistaken activities' to the customer.
6. Account information after completing the transaction is made available to the customer, which enhance the transparency in transaction, if any wrong operation

without the consent of the customer is informed within seconds, so that the grievances can be settled immediately.

7. The banks remind their customers with appropriate messages as per their requirements such as for their outstanding loan repayments.
8. Currency usage can be minimized in most of the transactions; from this the burden on the supply of the currency can be reduced.
9. On-line purchase of goods and services by the customers can be entertained with the help of 'internet' banking services.
10. This is a 'cost-free' service to the customer as no extra-amount is charged or deducted from the customer account.
11. Bank personal experience less rush over counter, where they can serve more for illiterate or age-old people.
12. The house-keeping activities of banking, automatically up-dated due to the computerized linkage between customer devices to the banking devices through inter-net

Despite of the above advantages have been experiencing both by the bank, and customer there some.

Challenges

Yet to be settled out for the risk-free environment for the above services:

1. The rural population in India is expected approximately spread across 600,000 villages; to them it is not possible to link with internet activity. Gradual in-take is possible in long run only.
2. There are many rules and regulations have to be adhered by both the bank, and the customer, which are laid down by the Reserve Bank of India. These rules also change time by time which consists little amount of risk in performing transactions.

3. It is not possible to transact when 'huge amount' of transaction involves. The bank prefers the personal interaction only.
4. So far the banks have been allowing Indian currency only. It is not possible to deal the transaction in foreign currency as the value of currency have been changing day-by-day, which leave lot of confusion in the minds of customer.
5. Literate customer only performs these 'hec-tech' operations, with lot of doubts in mind. According to the survey of Sri Prena Sharma Bamoriya and Dr. Preeti Sing in their article work named as "Mobile Banking in India: Barriers in adoption and Services Preferences: identified that, there are 87.87 percentage of bank account customer were availing mobile banking service from Public and Government banks. The State Bank of India was largest mobile banking service provider overall followed by Punjab National Bank. Among private banks ICICI Bank was leading in mobile banking services. It also expected that nearly 24.24 % of customer's avails mobile banking daily, and 45.25% people uses once it a 6 months. In this survey there are 86.9% of customers prefer to check their account balances, 65.2% of people for last transaction check, 60.8% for their bill payments, 30.4% for fund transfer, 26.1% for share trading, 21.7% for cheque book request and 8.6% were for their status check.

CONCLUSION

The banking operation of any country boosts the economic activity by co-coordinating the entire sector. The primary aspect the banks deals their business is the amount deposited by their respective customers. Their customer utmost satisfaction enables them to collect more cash from them. If new technology is adapted and uses with the defined rules and regulations by considering the technical restrictions will always provides the intended results. The mobile and inter-net banking operations so far yielding the greater benefits to the customer in India, by solving their tiny problem, these too can be minimized to zero level in near future. In near future one can see, all the Indian banking operations will be connected to safe electronic mode and can dealt globally. But steps should be taken to educated customers regarding use e-Banking system.

REFERENCES

Agarwal, R, Rastogi, S. & Mehrotra, A., "Customers perspectives regarding e-banking in an emerging economy, Journal of Retailing and Consumer Services, Vol. 16, pp. 340-351, 2009.

Andrew Musiime and Malinga Ramadhan–Internet banking, consumer adoption and customer satisfaction-African Journal of Marketing Management Vol. 3(10), pp. 261-269, October 2011.

Prema Sharma BamorYa, Dr. Preeti Singh—Mobile Banking in India: Barriers in Adoption and Service Preferences—Integra Review—A Journal of Management—Volume 5, No. 1 June, 2012, pp. 1-7.

Sharma, Prerna, & Singh, Preeti (2009). Users perception about mobile banking-with special reference to Indore & around. Review of Business & Technology Research, Vol. 2, 1, 1-4. Telecom Report (May 2010). TRAI, India.

Tiwari, Rajnish, & Stephan, Buse (2007). The Mobile Commerce Prospects: A Strategic Analysis of Opportunities in the Banking Sector. Retrieved from http://www. global-innovation.net/publications/PDF/HamburgUP_Tiwari_ Commerce.pdf.

Vyas, Charul (2009). Mobile banking in India-Perception and Statistics. Vital Analytics. Retrieved from http://www.telecomindiaonUne.com/telecom-india-dailv-telecom-station-mobile-banking-in-indig-perception-and-statistics.html.

E-Banking Management
Edited by: **Dr. Rabi N. Misra**
ISBN: 978-93-5056-788-3
Edition: **2016**
Published by: **Discovery Publishing House Pvt. Ltd., New Delhi (India)**

Innovation in Banking Sector (Kinds of Service Offered by Banks)

Dr. R.N. Misra
Prof. MBA, PGCMS, SMIT, BPUT
K. Janardhanudu
Lecturer in Commerce,
PSC & KVSC Government Degree College,
Nandyal, Kurnool Dist.

Introduction

The term Innovation means "to make something new". Banks have no longer restricted themselves to traditional banking activities, but explored new avenues to increase business and capture new markets. Right from the inception of RBI in 1935 to 1990 traditional banking activities took place. A bank customer would have been to bank with those who provided just with a fixed deposit or recurring deposit in addition to his savings account. Today there is a need to spread the wealth around, diversifying the savings into shares, mutual funds, pension products and insurance. Now a-days a banking sector plays a very important role in human life; banks motivate people to make saving money for their future. Banks provide number of facilities to the people, banking services has become a need of the society, banks have choice to offer all those as a part of their convenience banking to customers or lose him. So greater emphasis was placed on technology and innovation. Here I am trying to explain different types of innovations adopted by the banks.

Innovations in Banking Sector

1. **Saral Money:** Saral money, it is an innovative payment product, which ensures that everyone with am Aadhar number automatically has an Aadhar inked account in a bank, was launched by Chief Minister of Delhi, Sheila Dixit in December, 2012. People would be able to purchase the Saral money debit card across the counter from grocery shops and bank branches. It would facilitate instant account opening, and simplified documentation and accessibility to reach. The project has been launched in collaboration by the UIDAI and five banks viz. Axis Bank, HDFC Bank, ICICI, Indian Overseas Bank, and State Bank of India. This scheme would bring banking to the door steps of the citizens. The Delhi Government decided to implement cash transfer mode with the help of Aadhar number for its most ambitious Food Security Programme "Delhi Annashri Yojana". With Saral money the government and other institutions would be able to send money to anyone using only an Aadhar number, irrespective of whether the beneficiary has bank account or not, The beneficiary would be then able to withdraw money from any ATM or micro ATM using biometric authentication provided by Aadhar. By linking of Aadhar number with bank account, the Government can directly deposit the subsidy amount. Therefore it can eliminate the intermediaries and this ultimately reduces the corruption in Public Distribution System. By linking of Aadhar number with bank account and PAN card, we can minimize the tax evasion and this helps the Indian economy a lot.
2. **E-Banking:** E-banking enables people to carry out most of their banking transactions using safe website which is operated by the respected bank with the various

capabilities of the computer and other technological developments. The following are the advantages of electronic banking:

(*a*) It is very convenient as it can be used at home or office.

(*b*) It works for seven days a week and 24 hours a day.

(*c*) Payment of bills can also be handled properly and smartly.

(*d*) No longer required waiting in long queue.

Disadvantages

(*a*) Without Internet connection it is not possible to access account.

(*b*) Security of transactions is big issue. The account may be hacked by unauthorized people over Internet.

(*c*) Password security is must. Otherwise the account may be misused.

(*d*) Sometimes it is difficult to note whether the transaction was successful or not.

3. **Corporate Banking:** Corporate and investment banking provide financial services to large corporate and multinational companies. It provides the following services:

   (*a*) Overdraft Facility.

   (*b*) Domestic and International Payment.

   (*c*) Letters of Guarantee.

   (*d*) Working Capital facility for Domestic and International Trade.

4. **Rural Banking:** There is considerable gap between demand and supply for all financial services especially in rural segments. Almost 70% of Rural Population does not have bank account, 85% do not have credit card access, and 10% of people do not have any insurance. More importantly still 60% of rural poor people borrow from money lenders, friends and other sources. So it provides and regulates credit services for the promotion and

development of rural sector mainly agriculture, cottage and village industries, handicrafts etc. Of course the rural banks also have the following disadvantages:

(*a*) Profits are much lesser.

(*b*) Revenues are much lesser.

(*c*) Numbers of customers are lesser.

(*d*) The types of services provided are lesser.

5. **NRI Banking:** NRI stands for Non Resident Indian. It may be defined as a person who has lived out of India for a period not less than 180 days during previous year. NRI banking facility is exclusively designed for diverse banking requirements of the vast NRI population spreading across the globe. For NRIs two types of accounts are there. They are Non-resident External (NRE) account and Non-resident Ordinary (NRO) account.

   NRE account is allows only remittances in foreign currencies. The account can be retained in designated foreign currencies viz. US Dollars, Euro and Yen etc. Even the account holder has an account in India; rupees cannot be deposited, though it can be withdrawn in the form of rupee. NRO account is the account by a NRI, in which rupee as well as foreign currencies can be deposited, but withdrawal is allowed for rupees only. India has a lot of human resources and most of software employees going abroad. So if the banks put considerable interest in this area, they can be flourished.

6. **Mobile Banking:** Over the last few years, the mobile and wireless market has been one of the fastest growing markets in the world and it is still growing at a rapid pace. This opens up huge market for financial institutions interested in offering value added services. Due to the limitations of internet banking, mobile banking is emerged. It provides yet another channel for banking services. It is the hottest area of development in the banking sector and it is expected to replace online banking. In the past 5 years, the number of people using

mobile phones increased three times as compared to the use of debit or credit card holders. Moreover 85% to 90% of mobile users do not own credit cards.

The following are the advantages of Mobile Banking:

(*a*) It utilizes the mobile connectivity of telecom operators and therefore does not require an internet connection.

(*b*) We can check our account balance, review recent transactions, transfer funds, payment bills, manage investments etc.

(*c*) Mobile banking is available round the clock 24/7/365. So, it is convenienent for mobile phone owners of rural areas.

Disadvantages of Mobile Banking:

(*a*) Mobile banking users are at risk of receiving fake SMS messages and scams.

(*b*) The loss of a person's mobile device means that criminals can gain access to our mobile banking PIN and other sensitive information.

(*c*) Basic models of phone did not have mobile connectivity, so mobile banking is not available on these basic phones.

7. **Bio metric ATM's:** Bio metric ATM's will replace traditional ATM's across the country. A bio-metric ATM recognizes a customer not by an ATM card or a personal Id. Number but a customer himself is considered as an ATM card. The banks can authenticate Identity of customers with iris, or finger print or palm print. The first bio-metric ATM in India was installed by ICICI Bank in 2005 in Andhra Pradesh, The latest bio-metric ATM however examine the tiny veins located just beneath the surface of skin. According to studies bio-metric micro vein ATM's will only make a mistake one in approximately one million times. Even though bio-metric ATM's use advanced technology, they still have following disadvantages:

(*a*) The criminals could take finger or palm from the victim in order to steal or gain authorized access.

(*b*) If a person's body parts are damaged, or worse in an accident cannot be easily replaced like a forgotten password.

8. **NEFT and RTGS:** NEFT stands for National Electronic Fund Transfer. It is a system that operates on a Deferred Net Settlement (DNS) basis which settles transactions in batches. In DNS the settlement takes place with all transactions received till the particular cut off time. Generally NEFT operates on hourly batches. Ex: there are 12 settlements from 8 am to 7 pm on week days and six settlements from 8 am to 1 pm on Saturdays. Any transaction initiated after a designated settlement time would have to wait till the next designated settlement time. RTGS stands for Real Time Gross Settlement system. It is a fund transfer mechanism where transfer of money takes place from one bank to another on a 'real time' and gross basis. Considering that the funds settlement takes place in the books of the Reserve Bank of India, the payments are final and irrevocable. The RTGS system is primarily meant for large value transactions. The minimum amount to be remitted through RTGS is ₹ 2 lakhs and no upper ceiling for RTGS transactions. For this purpose IFSC code for beneficiary bank is required. IFSC codes is available on the RBI website (http://rbidocs.rbi.org.in/rdocs/RTGS/docs/RTGEB0112.xls)

CONCLUSION

Whatever the technology is advanced and innovations in Banking Sector, it Should helpful to the customer as an individual and the Bank. It will speed the work and provide service to the customer as and when necessary without wasting time and energy.

E-Banking Management
Edited by: Dr. Rabi N. Misra
ISBN: 978-93-5056-788-3
Edition: 2016
Published by: Discovery Publishing House Pvt. Ltd.,
New Delhi (India)

Technological Innovation in Indian Commercial Banks

R. Umadevi
Osmania University,
Hyderabad

Introducton

A well developed banking system is necessary for economic development of our country. Banks mobilize savings from the public and provide them for economic development. Banks provide number of services to the society. Traditionally banking meant borrowing and lending but now a day's banks are providing very innovative services. Indian banking sector has already undergone a huge transformation in the years since Independence. After the implementation of LPG Policy the Indian banking sector has seen a lot of changes provide better quality services to the customers. Banks began to use technology to improve their efficiency. The Indian banking system has changed with the introduction of innovative techniques like ATMs, Tele banking, Internet banking etc. The Indian banking sector was moving rapidly towards Universal banking. The technology of banks is fast changing with the move of time. The technology transformation in banking is getting into new wave of business focused innovations. Technology transformation has been playing a key role in enabling changes. Today we see the various technological platforms used by banks for the conduct of day-to-day operations.

Objectives

- To study the technological innovations in Indian commercial banks.
- To analyze the technology innovations in public sector banks.
- To analyze the technology innovations in private sector banks.

Research Methodology

The present study is based on the secondary data collected from various journals, books and published data from RBI (Reserve Bank of India). The present study is confined to know the technology innovations in Indian commercial banks. The scheduled commercial banks consist public sector banks, private sector banks and foreign banks. The present paper mainly aims to analyze the technology innovations in public sector and private sector banks.

Technology Innovations in Indian Commercial Banks

The technology evolution of Indian banking sector has been largely directed by the various committees set-up by Reserve Bank of India. Technology has played a very important role in banking sector. Technology now allows these banks are working on the concept of 24 hrs in 7 days working made possible due to Tele banking, ATMs, Internet Banking, Mobile Banking and E-banking. These technology innovations are used to reach maximum customers at lower cost and in most efficient manner. The effect of these banking innovations puts both banker and customer get a lot of benefits. In the Indian context, technological innovation and investment in IT during the period 2005-06 to 2009-10 led to efficiency gains for the scheduled commercial banks.

The Reserve Bank has continued to focus on increasing the acceptance and penetration of safe, secure and efficient non-cash payment modes comprising cheque, credit/debit cards, and transactions through ECS/RTGS/NEFT, over the years. When the business and commercial tends in the process of electronic banking, it covers any form of business including banking. The popular electronic delivery channels are the following:

- ATMs
- Smart Cards
- Tele Banking
- Internet Banking
- Real Time Gross Settlement System

ATMs

ATM (Automatic Teller Machine) card is very useful to a cardholder in an emergency to withdraw cash from banks even they are closed. ATMs are an issue of survival for the banks and are becoming just another part of everyday life. Falling costs of machines and connectivity is a key factor contributing to the growth of ATM network. There are more then 35,000 offsite and onsite ATMs are available. At the end of June 2007 there are 28,704 ATMs are available and at the end of 2008 June 36, 314 ATMs are available. During 2011-12, an additional 21,000 ATMs were deployed by the banks. By this we can understand the uses and preference of ATMs in public.

Table 1: ATMs of scheduled Commercial Banks.

(as at end of march 2012)

Sl. No.	Bank group	On-site ATMs	Off-site ATMs	Total number of ATMs
1.	Public sector banks	34,012	24,181	58,193
2.	Private sector banks	13,249	22,830	36,079
3.	Foreign banks	284	1,130	1,414
	All SCBs	47,545	48,141	95,684

Real Time Gross Settlement (RTGS) System

The inter Bank Payments handle large amounts of money. The RTGS system is one in which payment instructions between banks are processed and settled individually and continuously throughout the day. In India currently it covers more than 28,000 branches of banks. The attraction of RTGS is that the payee banks and their customers receive funds with certainty and finality during the same day enabling them to use the funds immediately without exposing themselves to risk. RTGS system, do not create credit risk for the receiving participant because they settle the each payment individually, as soon as it is accepted , liquidity risks remains, as well as the possibility of the risks being shifted outside the system. The security has to ensure that hacking is not possible at the site.

Smart Cards

The smart card technology is also widely used by the bankers to market their products. It is more secure than ATMs, credit cards and debit cards. Because card related frauds and crimes cannot take place in smart cards. It provides communication security as it verifies whether the sign is genuine or not.

Tele-banking

Tele banking is increasingly used as a delivery channel for marketing banking services. A customer can do entire non-cash related banking over the phone anywhere at any time.

Electronic Funds Transfer (EFTs)

Electronic funds transfer is an electronic debit of the customer's account at the point of sales of goods and services in the market. Bank customer uses his credit and debit cards for his purchases. This is a system whereby anyone who wants to make payment to another person or another company, can approach his bank and make cash payment.

Internet Banking

Internet banking is also known as online banking. It is the latest wave in information technology. All the services that the bank has permitted on the internet are displayed in menu. Internet banking is a platform for electronic delivery of banking. The customer can perform various banking functions. Such as:

- Checking account balance.
- Making account enquiry.
- Ordering a demand.
- Requesting a check book.
- Transferring funds.
- Opening additional deposit accounts.

CONCLUSION

The above study technology innovation in Indian commercial banks is reveals that technology has played effective role to reach the customer satisfaction. At present almost every banks are using technology in their daily banking transactions. In the process of implementing technology innovations they have started ATM facilities, Real Time Gross Settlement System, Tele-banking, Internet banking etc. The present study concluded that the banking sector changes occurred rapidly with the introduction of various innovations.

REFERENCES

Avasthi, G.P.M. (2000-01), "Information Technology in Banking: Challenges for Regulators", Prajnan, Vol. XXIX.

Financial Services—Banking and Insurance (2013), Himalaya Publishing House.

Metzer, S.R. (2000), "Strategic Planning for Future Bank growth", The Banker's Magazone (July August).

Pathrose P.P. (2001), "Hi Tech. Banking Prospects and Problem", IBA Bulletin, Vol. XXII (July).

Priyanka "Technology-Future in Banking" in banking in the new millennium by R.K.Uppal, Rimpi Kaur.

Report on Trend and progress of commercial banks in India 2011-12.

E-Banking Management
Edited by: Dr. Rabi N. Misra
ISBN: 978-93-5056-788-3
Edition: 2016
Published by: Discovery Publishing House Pvt. Ltd., New Delhi (India)

Role of Information Technology in Indian Banking Sector

Dr. B. Sakunthala
Lecturer in Commerce,
Government Degree College, Karveti Nagaram

Introduction

Financial sector in general and banking industry in particular is the largest spender and beneficiary from Information Technology. This endeavors to relate the international trends in it with the Indian banking industry. Banking in India has passed through several phases since the times when formal banking activity has commenced. Off all, the current phase is the most interesting one where technology is playing a predominant role in deciding the acceptability or otherwise of a particular Bank to the customer. The banking industry is highly information-intensive. No wonder banks globally have been effectively deploying Information Technology as a strategic resource to achieve speed, efficiency, cost reduction, customer service and competitive advantage. In India, it was the new-generation banks that set the trend by using technology to the hilt. They brought in anywhere, anytime, anyway banking to customers, the value proposition of the convenient, innovative, technology-enabled products and delivery channels attracted new, profitable customers to their fold in large numbers. Slowly, the traditional banks also realized the power of technology and initiated the absorption of technology to retain their profitable customers, and to enhance their efficiency, productivity and competitiveness.

Impact of Technology in Banking

Technology has enabled banks to overcome the barriers of time and space in extending their services to customers. The new technology-driven channels like internet banking, ATMs, EFT (Electronic Fund Transfer), debit cards, mobile banking, tele-banking, etc., are accessible to customers across the world. The value proposition to customers through these innovative channels has been tremendous. With automation, banks could offer their customers speed and convenience through single window service, extend business hours and provide anywhere, anytime banking. Self-service channels like ATMs, tele-banking and Net-banking are increasingly being used by customers.

This gives the bank personnel more time, which they can devote to business planning and development, recovery of loans and devising innovative delivery systems to serve customers. Also, in the modern market economy of fierce competition, technology facilitates each player to have its own unique products and services for competitive advantage.

Banks have to live with thinning margins these days and it is vital for them to reduce transaction costs. The new technology-driven channels greatly help them in this regard as the cost of transaction in the new delivery channels is only a fraction of what it was when they were done over the branch counter. For instance, a counter transaction is a typical bank branch may incur a cost of ₹ 50 to 60, while it is only around ₹ 15 to 20 if done through ATM. The cost will come down further if transactions are done through a Point of Sale (POS) terminal or the Internet. Thus, it is imperative for banks to drive the customers to the new channels for controlling their transaction costs.

The heavy initial investment involved in infusing technology will be a major constraint for many banks. Also, one of the main constraints faced by traditional banks is the inadequate infrastructure in rural areas where they have branches in large numbers. For achieving maximum effectiveness, the technology solutions should be in alignment with the business requirements of the banks. As each organization has its own unique operational style, it has to be analyzed properly before opting for a technology solution which might be running successfully elsewhere. Also, all the necessary re-engineering of the process has to be done prior to fully automating any system for deriving the best fruits of technology. However, this is one of the toughest challenges for any traditional banks in India. An important aspect of any technology solution is its cost-effectiveness and the return on investment. Many a times, innovative technical solutions that are cost-effective can be developed in-house. However, this requires a dedicated team of technical and domain experts within the bank. Perhaps, the over-hyped 'outsourcing' model has to be re-examined in the context of banks in the country where the cost factor may be much more if an IT project is outsourced. From the information security angle also, in-house development is the ideal answer.

Banking has emerged as one of the riskiest business. Information is the lifeblood for banks in mitigating and managing risks. In the near future, banks have to gear up for Basel II compliance. This requires lots of information and knowledge management on the part of banks. However, the new technologies can come to the rescue of banks as never before in knowledge management. Collection, compilation, analysis and retrieval of massive data had never been so easy. With the explosive spread of the Internet and Web technologies, it is much easier to provide access to information to users 'anywhere, anytime'. For a successful banking business, management and analysis of large data and information play key roles in devising new strategies, products and services. With the cost of technology falling and their capacities increasing day-by-day, data warehousing has become affordable. Banks should set-up their own intranets and extranets, which will be a boon to both employees and customers, spread over wide geographic locations.

Need for IT Adoption in Banking

Information Technology has a significant influence on the banking sector. In fact, it started a new era in the banking operation. The application of IT in banks reduced the scope of conventional banking with manual operations. The banking sector is still undergone changes with innovation. It seems several lessons have emerged in the banking on account of this magical technology. Some important lessons in the contacts of IT with reference to banking sector are listed below :

- The increase in investment in banking sector has forced to switch on to automation of existing processes.
- Cost sharing between customers and products and its analysis forced banks to go for IT. Costs in banking are shared across products and even across customers. An investment that might have a positive impact on one customer base or product may have the desired impact on the overall cost base.
- Banking services may be a class of services for which demand and supply creates additional demand. Banks have recognized that they need to offer the conveniences of newer technology to retain their existing customers.
- The mix effect of technology in banking reflect the fact that technology can replace simple repetitive functions such as the basic calculations and internally oriented back office support functions that were automated initially.

Therefore, investment in new technology must be made to modernize the existing banks operations. The adoption of Information Technology also helps them to face competition and new challenges to meet the customer expectation in the contacts of globalization.

Initiatives by Government of India

The Government of India (GOI) is endeavoring to bring in more transparency in the public dealing department and has initiated various Mission Model Projects (MMP) under their e-governance plan. The banking division in the Ministry of Finance, GOI is making all out efforts to implement and monitor the success of initiatives proposed under the MMP for integration of core IT infrastructure of Public Sector Banks (PSBs) under the e-governance plan of the GOI. Broadly, the following two major projects pertaining to the banking industry are being considered under the e-governance plan of the GOI:

(*i*) **One India One Account :** The evolution of core banking technology in the country has put of the public and private sector banks at a standard technology platform which is scaleable and interoperable. In the implementation of Core Banking Solutions. (CBS) and induction of electronic channels, the Indian banking industry has empowered banks to launch newer products and services at par with those of the private sector banks. It has transformed the customer of the branch to the customer of the bank.

The next logical step initiated under the e-governance plan envisages integration of different core banking solutions deployed by various banks, thus creating mega-pool of centralized database of customers of different banks. With this, the customer of one bank shall eventually be able to transact his account from any other bank thus encouraging the concept of customer of the bank to the customer of the nation.

(*ii*) **Electronic Mass Payment System (EMPS):** Electronic mode of payments using smart card and Point of Sale (POS) terminals shall be viable alternative to paper based cash transactions of small value (micro-payments) to reduce the circulation of cash. Following concepts can be used for the EMPS :

Offline Smart Cards : A retailer or a merchant can install a machine for transaction of smart card. These machines would be used for transferring money from the customer's card to the retailer's.

Online Debit Cards: These are smart cards which may be linked to the bank accounts of the card holders and can be used in ATMs for cash withdrawals, fund transfers, etc., and at merchant establishment for online payments against purchases.

Formation of an ATM Corporation of India

Presently various banks are installing offsite ATMs in adjacent shops/establishments and we can find multiplicity of ATMs in a busy market place. In order to ensure optimum utilization of ATMs and to avoid repetitive and wasteful expenses being made by the banks, there is a need to form an autonomous "ATM Corporation of India". Various banks can get together and transfer the management of ATMs to this autonomous body which may deal in activities such as cash replacement, site management, security and also procurement of ATM machines and other related hardware to get price benefits on mass purchases. Instead of each bank issuing the ATM card, a standard card operable and acceptable at each ATM can be introduced. The shareholding pattern and profit sharing of the new autonomous company can be based on number of ATMs being transferred by each bank. The RBI has already initiated steps towards rationalizing charges on the use of inter-bank ATMs which are finally aimed to be brought to NIL by the end March 2009.

Real Time Gross Settlement (RTGS)

The Reserve Bank of India (RBI) has already implemented Real Time Gross Settlement (RTGS). RTGS will provide for a new generation of high value payment systems that will enable the core of the banking system across the country make secure inter bank payment across the country. These transactions will cover all general transactions and central account of the RBI, including the banks general ledger. This process can be effectively implemented only when all banks implement CBS. The implementation of CBS followed an interesting pattern in 2003-04 when most private sector and Multi National Corporation (MNC) banks and even large PSBs adopted the system. Therefore, it is the turn of the remaining smaller PSBs banks as well as the co-operative banks still in the Total Branch Automation (TBA) phase to go in for core banking with a vengeance3. With RBI directives necessitating the adoption of centralized solutions, many banks that are yet to adopt CBS have opted atleast for consolidated MIS solutions. This is particularly true for a number of smaller co-operative banks for whom core banking product solutions are ex-orbitantly priced at Rs. 5 to 8 crore. As per the latest guidelines of the Central Vigilance Commission (CVC), major business of a bank's branches should be done in a computerized environment and in this light CBS will act as tool to check fraud and other inimical activities. Besides, in view of the proposed mergers and consolidations, banks should be compatible so that there will be no operational problems.

Internet Banking: Indian Scenario

In India, slowly but steadily, the Indian customer is moving towards Internet Banking. A number of banks have either adopted Internet banking or are on the threshold of adopting it. The banks started Internet banking initially with simple function such as getting information about interest rates, checking account balances and computing loan eligibility. Then the services were extended to online bill payment, transfer of funds between accounts and cash management services for corporate. Recently, banks have started to facilitate payment for e-commerce transactions by directly debiting bank accounts or through credit cards. It will add to the revenues of the banks.

Internet Banking : Issues

The main issues in Internet Banking today relate to security, authentication, non-repudiation, privacy, trust, internet banking business continuance plan, security awareness and security breach detection and reporting etc., they are not only relevant for the banks but for satisfaction and confidence of the customers. The objective must be to provide a robust and reliable technological platform, which ensures authentication, non-repudiation, availability of services, integrity and confidentiality of data and transaction, trust and privacy:

Security: In Internet Banking security is considered as an asset and so worthy protection. Security concerns in the Internet scenario manifest in the use of public network and related security threats online. The bank should put in place proper and tested IT infrastructure and software.

Authentication: User authentication assumes a great significance in Internet banking as customers log on to the system from different locations without any physical means of authentication. Therefore, proper identification and authentication procedures should be established and followed to establish accountability and to prevent unauthorized persons from gaining access to the systems. This can be achieved through, for example, passwords or smart tokens; logical access controls to establish who has access to a specific type of information resources and the type of access permitted.

Non-Repudiation: The non-repudiation issue is one of the most important issues in online banking. No customer should later claim that any particular transaction was to transacted by him/her. Thus, proper authentication and authorization mechanism using encryption and digital signature should be established.

Privacy: The bank should provide privacy of data and the transaction in all circumstances except in cases when instructed by the competent legal authority or the government to divulge the same. Even if the website of database maintenance is outsourced, the bank should take the primary responsibility of preventing breach of confidentiality. Thus, privacy not only covers confidentiality of the banks data but also guarantees the data's level of privacy, which is being used by different operators at different levels of authorization.

Availability: The Internet banking services should be available round-the-clock to the customers or else the goodwill the reputation of the bank will take a beating resulting in financial loss as well as losing out loyal customers. The system should be up and running in reliable manner when needed and timely access to resources should be ensured all the time.

System Architecture and Design: The choice of technological infrastructure generally determines the success of Internet banking in the long run. A correct system architecture and design will help in managing operational and security risks to a greater extent. The banking services can also be catered in a reliable fashion. The bank should take care that any financial transaction should move only in a secure environment.

Trust: In Internet Banking establishment of trust among the parties is essential. This can be established through a trusted third party designated as a Certification Authority (CA). The digital certificates issued by the CA to various entries along with at least two factor identification mechanisms can be trusted for the authentication and non-repudiation of the users and transactions in internet banking.

Business Continuity Planning: The business continuity planning should be an integral part of banks internet banking policy. It ensures that the bank can prevent interruptions, and recover and resume processing in the event of a partial or completed interruption internet banking system/services availability. A long day in making available the services to the customers in case of disruption of internet banking system may erode the banks credibility and goodwill as well as the customer's confidence in the banks internet banking services.

Security awareness, training, and education: The purpose of creating awareness towards information security in the area of Internet Banking through training and education is necessary for understanding the need of information security, protection of passwords, awareness of various spy wares and malicious codes. Advanced training for the system administrators may also be conducted to optimally configure the Internet Banking system and update them about the latest threats being present in the Internet Banking domain.

Security breach detection and Incidence Response System: One major area of concern today in Internet Banking is the timely detection of security breach and incident response mechanism to perform the necessary damage control exercise. Follow up and exception reporting of logs like audit log, system log, users log, etc., become important tasks. Responsibilities and accountability of the key personnel along with other staff members should be clearly demarcated.

E-Banking Management
Edited by: Dr. Rabi N. Misra
ISBN: 978-93-5056-788-3
Edition: 2016
Published by: Discovery Publishing House Pvt. Ltd., New Delhi (India)

Efficiency in Electronic Banking

Dr. R.N. Misra
Prof. MBA, PGCMS, SMIT, BPUT

Dr. Rama Krishna
Lecturer in Commerce,
P.R. Government College (A),
Kakinada-533 001

Introduction

The banking industry has become stronger after the deep crisis of the eighties and it has been experiencing an increasing concentration through mergers of large and medium size banks. As it is today we found five large banks (with a market share of 10% and above), eight banks with a market share between 2% and 6% and twelve small banks (with a market share below 1%). Several of these banks are established as open corporations (54% of total banks remain as branches of international banks. Another characteristic of the banking industry is the adequate level of solvency and the good supervision and prudential regulation from the economic authority.

The strength of the banking system was tested with the "tequila effect" in 1994 and the recent Asian crisis. Until today the system is working and all the banks have fulfilled the liquidity, solvency and capitalization requirements. Nevertheless, there is always a concern related to the efficiency reached by the banks. Especially when one of the reasons given by the owners to merge two banks is efficiency. This paper analyzes the bank efficiency and its determinants using both profit and cost function. During the last 5 years, the Internet has brought about fundamental changes in the rules of operation of the banking industry (Gunasekaran and Love, 1999). Specifically, the industry has moved rapidly to exploit the new communication/transaction channels offered by the Internet to improve their front-end Internet applications. As a result, the number of e-banklng Websites has increased rapidly (Aladwani, 2001). Currently, there are more than 11,250 e-banking sites located worldwide. In Iran alone, for example, more than 25 online banking sites are available with all of them to presentation Services.

Service Quality in e-banking

Today, many financial services organizations are endeavoring to become customer focused. A key component of improved customer focus is the implementation of tools that allow development of better relations between banks and their customers (customer-bank relationship). Across all service industries, service quality remains a critical issue as businesses strive to maintain a comparative advantage in the marketplace (Kandampully and Duddy, 1999). Because financial services, particularly banks, compete in the marketplace with generally undifferentiated roducts, service quality becomes the primary competitive weapon (Stafford, 1996; Kirn et al., 1998). Easing wood and Storey (1993) report that total quality is the most important factor in the success of new financial services. Likewise, Bennett and Higgins (1988) believe that a competitive edge in banking originates almost exclusively from service quality. In general, it is conceded that banks that excel in quality service have a distinct marketing edge because improved levels of service quality relate to higher revenues, increased cross-sell ratios, higher customer retention (Bennett and Higgins, 1988), and an expanded market share (Bowen and Hedges, 1993). As discussed above, providing quality service and products to customers is essential for success and survival in today's competitive banking environment (Wang et al., 2003). Quality products and services enhance a bank's reputation, improve its customer retention, attract new customers, and increase its financial performance and Profitability.

Quality Function E-Banking

QFD is a systematic process used by cross-functional teams to identify and resolve the issues involved in providing products, processes, services, and strategies that enhance customer satisfaction (Gonza'lez et al., 2003). Akao (1990) defines QFD as a method for defining design qualities that are in keeping with customer expectations and then translating the customer requirements into design targets and critical quality assurance points that can be used throughout the production/service development phase Gonza'lez (2001) states that QFD has two fundamental purposes to improve (1) the communication of customer requirements throughout the organization, and (2) the completeness of specifications and to make them traceable directly to customer requirements and needs. Some uniform rules concerning the use of electronic signatures and records in retail and commercial transactions may emerge as a result of recent changes in federal law. While these changes provide more legal certainty that may help promote the growth of electronic commerce, federal law leaves unresolved several important issues related to the validity of an electronic record, as well as the verification and authorization of parties who conduct electronic transactions. In addition, the Automated Clearing House (ACH) system is increasingly being used as a payment system for funds transfers initiated on the Internet.

Literature Review on Service Quality in e-banking

As a consequence of the increasing importance of modern information and communication technologies for the delivery of financial services the analysis of e-banking quality issues becomes an area of growing interest to researchers and managers (Hughes, 2003; Jayawardhena, 2004). Virtually all studies dealing with the quality of electronic financial services focus on specific aspects of the quality evaluation. To our knowledge, the study presented by Gounaris and Dimitriadis (2003) is the first attempt to investigate the service quality of e-banking portals. Based on the SERVQUAL, the author identifies three quality dimensions, namely customer care and risk reduction benefit, information benefit and interaction facilitation. These dimensions are represented by only 14 items, a fact that has to be criticized. These indicators do not fully cover all relevant facets regarding the business activities of an e-banking portal, which contradicts the idea of portals as holistic business models. For example, aspects like offering a broad spectrum of complementary products and services or the reliability of service delivery are not included. In the article, the author explores the implementation techniques of Activity-Based Costing in the banking sector on the example of an Estonian bank3 in order to analyze the cost structure for traditional and electronic channel transactions. Also conclusions are drawn about the profitability of e-banking transactions.

Definition

The Internet includes all related web-enabling technologies and open telecommunication networks ranging from direct dial-up, the public World Wide Web, cable, and virtual private networks (BIS-EBG, 2003) Internet banking (e-banking) is defined to include the provision of retail and small value banking products and services through electronic channels as well as large value electronic payments and other wholesale banking services delivered electronically. (BIS-EBG, 2003)—Basic information e-banking/web sites that just disseminate information on banking products and services offered to bank customers and the general public;—Simple transactional e-banking/web sites that allow bank customers to submit applications for different services, make queries on their account balances, and submit instructions to the bank, but do no permit any account transfers; Advanced transactional e-banking/web sites that allow bank customers to electronically transfer funds to/from their accounts pay bills, and conduct other banking transaction online. Usually, e-banking refers to types II and III.

Internet Profit Generation

E-commerce, when properly integrated into existing banking operations, can lead to substantial cost savings and higher profitability. Cost savings occur by virtue of automating customer transactions such as funds transfers, payments, account balance inquiries, etc. Strategic alliances with insurance companies, mortgage companies, and stock brokerage firms can lead to additional business opportunities that otherwise will go unrealized. Furthermore, banks are able to retain customers more effectively when offering services that are value-added. This has been clearly demonstrated in the case of Wells Fargo Bank. When customers moved online with Wells Fargo, the percentage of customers taking their business elsewhere dropped 50 per cent. As a result of these positive experiences with online banking, one in six of the bank's new customers are referrals from existing customers. And, thus, did not cost the bank anything to acquire them (Meckbach, 1999).

Benefits of Internet and E-banking to Banks

Cost Savings Orr (1999) states that electronic processing dramatically reduces the cost per transaction. According to DiDio (1998), the average transaction cost at a full service bank is about $1.07. It reduces to $0.27 at an ATM and falls to about a penny if the same transaction is conducted on the web. Also, there are opportunities for banks to present customer bills electronically. The cost of delivering bills electronically is substantially ower than if the bill was in paper form delivered through the mail. Irvine (1999) states that electronic bill presentment costs 40% less than paper delivery. These cost savings can offer customers and banks alike reduced cost of banking and still provide efficient and varied services.

Customer Satisfaction

Retention is increasingly developing into key success factors in e-banking. Most importantly, profitable e-banking requires a strong focus not only on the acquisition of new customers but also on the retention of existing customers, since the acquisition costs in online banking exceed that of traditional off line business by 20-40 per cent (Reibstein, 2002; Reichheld and Schefter, 2000). Consequently, establishing long-term customer relationships is a prerequisite for generating positive customer value on the internet. The most important step in providing a sophisticated level of service through e-banking portals is to identify and measure the dimensions of portal quality. This is the basic prerequisite for an effective quality management. Thereby, a portal's market success greatly depends on a customer-oriented definition of quality. What really determines an e-banking portal's quality is the customers' expectations and demands rather than objective or technical characteristics (Zeithaml et al., 2002). Therefore, in the following, we develop a model for assessing quality from the user's perspective.

The Role of e-channels in the Banking Sector

Electronic banking (e-banking) is the newest delivery channel of banking services. The definition of e-banking varies amongst researches partially because electronic banking refers to several types of services through which a bank's customers can request information and carry out most retail banking services via computer, television or mobile phone (Daniel, 1999; Mols, 1998; Sathye, 1999). Burr, 1996, for example, describes it as an electronic connection between the bank and customer in order to prepare, manage and control financial transactions. Electronic banking can also be defined as a variety of the following platforms: (*a*) Internet banking (or online banking), (*b*) telephone banking, (*c*) TV-based banking, (*d*) mobile phone banking, and (*e*) PC are banking (or offline banking). In this paper, the ATM (Automated Teller Machine) channel is also added to the research.

Account Origination and Customer Verification

With the growth in electronic banking and commerce, financial institutions need to utilize reliable methods of originating new customer accounts online. Customer identity verification during account origination is important in reducing the risk of identity theft, fraudulent account applications, and unenforceable account agreements or transactions. Potentially significant risks arise when a financial institution accepts new customers through the Internet or other purely electronic channel because of the absence of the physical cues that bankers traditionally use to identify individuals.

To summarize these assumptions, the following can be stated:

1. It is possible to implement ABC in the banking sector, although the calculations system can become overly detailed to manage.
2. Electronic channels provide cost-saving for banks and their clients. In the case of Hans bank, Online bank payments are 12.5 times cheaper and offline bank payments are 30 times cheaper than the traditional transactions made in the branch Network.
3. The decrease in transaction costs is slower than expected.

The reason for this is that the existing channels cannot be closed at the same speed as new distribution channels are introduced and funds invested in their development and maintenance. As the number of transactions in branches has been steadily decreasing, the unit cost expenses related to branch transactions will increase the branches will become more focused on consulting and problem-solving than on regular transaction processing (payments, cash operations). The initial investments in e-channels IT and security solutions were high, also IT and product development require major investment at the beginning stage. We can conclude that e-channels transactions will probably become more cost-efficient for banks in a few years' time. The detailed information provided by the ABC technique can help banks to; regulate and reduce some cost components. Understanding of the IT cost components of e-banking distribution channels gives an insight about the fixed and floating components of IT expenses and thus can create the pre-conditions for cost saving.

Online Banking in Iran like Country

The development of online banking in Iran country reveals some common traits. In recent years, the dominant industrial strategy in Iran country is for banking groups to own both pure internet banks and more traditional banks with an internet portal, thus exploiting both business models. Internet banks that initially offered only online tools have gone over to a mixed model, using other channels as, for example, telephone banking, or financial advisors. Stand-alone internet banks are rather rare. The large majority of traditional banks have set-up an internet portal to diversify their distribution channel. But in addition, many banking groups have set-up separate internet banks with their own brand that function as independent entities. We examine the performance of banking groups that have set-up internet banks (pure internet banks) versus banks that offer a mix of distribution channels (mixed banks). We look into the development of online banking in all cities Iran country. This enables us to expand the dataset to produce clearer evidence regarding the performance of online banking. But in addition, it allows us to contrast different banking models. This makes the results more widely applicable than studies focused on a specific market. These cities not only represent a variety of banking structures but also differ in their economic structure, and in particular in their adoption of new technologies. These external factors possibly affect the success of internet banking.

Prospects Impact of E-banking on Traditional Banking

The early conventional wisdom: Internet banking would destroy the traditional banking business model and promote the entry of newcomers from the outside of the banking industry. Developing countries could have the "opportunities to leapfrog" in the adoption of e-finance on a large scale. In reality, e-banking develops fast, but not damaging as conventional wisdom projected. The notion of leapfrog has not worked in many developing countries due to various impediments. This can be verified by UNCTAD report. "Some positive signs are already visible, including a high level of acceptance of technology by customers and financial institutions....H (h) however; most projects have not yet been deployed on a large scale." (UNCTAD 2002. It provides a comprehensive look at the status of e-finance in developing countries. It covers arrange of areas related to e-finance including e-banking, e-payments, e-trades, and e-credit information).

Trust as a Function of Degree of Perceived Risk

Risk has been called element that gives the trust dilemma. If there was no risk and actions could be taken with complete certainly no trust would be needed. This element of risk is particularly pronounced in electronic commerce as opposed to traditional commerce. Previous research on trust lacks on clarifying the relationship of trust and risk. Although numerous authors have recognized the importance of risk to understand trust, no consensus on its relationship with trust exists. Trust is interwoven with risk, because it reduces the risk of falling victim to opportunistic behaviour.

Perceived Security

Security is being defined as a threat creates circumstance, condition, or event with the potential to cause economic hardship to data or network resources in the form of destruction, disclosure, modification of data, denial of service, and/or fraud, waste, and abuse. Under this definition, in the context of electronic banking threats can be made either through network and data transaction attacks or through unauthorized access to the account by means of false or defective authentication. Perceived security then is the customer's perception of the degree of protection against these threats. (Kalakota and Whinston, 1997).

Perceived Privacy

Privacy has been identified to be a major, if not the most critical, important to e-commerce: In our view, the single, overwhelming barrier to rapid growth of e-commerce is a lack of consumer trust that consumer protection and privacy laws will apply in cyberspace. Consumers worry, deservedly, that supposedly legitimate companies will take advantage of them by invading their privacy to capture information about them for marketing and other secondary purposes without their informed consent. A number of researchers have examined the concept of privacy from a behavioural perspective.

Perceived Trustworthiness

People make important buying decisions based, in part, on their level of trust in the product, salesperson, or the company. Similarly, electronic banking decision involves trust not simply on the transaction medium but also between the customer and the bank or the financial service provider.

CONCLUSION

This paper studies economic efficiency in the E-banking industry using a stochastic frontier approach. For measuring economic efficiency we used two indicators the cost and the alternative profit function. We found that banks that are open corporations tend to be more efficient in cost and profit than those banks that are branches of international banks. This result survives after controlling by size, market concentration, credit risk and economic activity. This would suggest two alternative hypotheses. The first one is related to principal agent problem. Banks, which are open corporations, are being observed closely by the market and they could be subject to take over. Therefore managers carefully handle cost and profit. On the other side foreign owners of banks, which are branches of multinational banks, tend to exert less control over the managers, with the corresponding cost and profit inefficiency. The second hypothesis is related to the type of business that these two groups are conducting. On the one hand, open corporations tend to be large banks that act as universal banks, by providing all the services permitted by the law. On the other hand, international branches tend to be small banks that are not involved in retailing banking and they are serving only to very large companies or they just do intermediate investment. Another finding supports the fact that principal agent problem is important for cost and profit efficiency is the evidence presented here on the relationship between ownership structure and efficiency.

REFERENCES

Akao, Y. (1990), Quality Function Deployment: Integrating Customer Requirements into Product Design, Productivity Press, and Cambridge, MA.

Aladwani, A.M. (2001), "Online banking: a field study of driverst, development challenges, and expectations", International Journal of Information Management, Vol. 21, pp. 213-25.

Bennett, D. and Higgins, M. (1988), "Quality means more than smiles", ABA Banking journal, Vol.46.

Bowen, J. and Hedges, R.B. (1993), "Increasing service quality in retail banking", Journal of Retail Banking, Vol. 15.

BIS 2003, Management and supervision of cross-border electronic banking activities.

Daniel, E. "Provision of electronic banking in the UK and Ireland," International Journal of Bank Marketing, 17, 2, 1999, pp. 72-82. "The Dynamo of E-Banking", Business Week Online, April 16, 2001.

Hughes, T. (2003), "Marketing challenges in e-banking: standalone or integrated?" Journal of Marketing Management, Vol. 19, pp. 1067-85.

E-Banking Management
Edited by: Dr. Rabi N. Misra
ISBN: 978-93-5056-788-3
Edition: 2016
Published by: Discovery Publishing House Pvt. Ltd., New Delhi (India)

Growth of Retail Electronic Payments in India

Dr. R.N. Misra
Prof. MBA, PGCMS, SMIT, BPUT

Dr. K. Sudarsan
Assistant Professor,
Dept. of MBA, SITAMS, Chittoor

Introduction

A payment is the transfer of wealth from one parry (person or company) to another. A payment system is usually made in exchange for the provision of goods, services or both, or to fulfill a legal obligation. The simplest and oldest form of payment is barter, the exchange of one good or service for another. In the modern world, common means of payment by an individual include money, cheque, debit, credit or bank transfer, and in trade such payments are frequently preceded by an invoice or result in a receipt. Payment system is a key component of any economic activity and financial system in any county. Efficient payments are essential for timely and secure completion of financial transactions, as well as movement of money. Electronic payment is the term used for any kind of payment processed without using cash or papers. Forms of electronic payment include used of Automated Clearing House (ACH), e-checks, direct debit, debit cards, and credit cards.

Cash and cheques are dominating in the Indian payments market. Currency is still a popular instrument in retail transactions in India due to convenience and the completeness of the transaction. The same could be a disadvantage when it comes to carrying large amount of cash (security risk) and making large-value payments. Cheques, on the other hand, are the next popular mode of payment and fund transfers. These are the potential transactions for conversion to the electronic payments segment.

Need for the Present Study

India is fast developing at a global level. But when looked inside, there are social evils which are deeply entrenched hindering the nation from growth. There are tiny aspects when noticed at the macro-level might not actually seem to make a difference. When implemented at the micro, one could see the difference very clearly. One such aspect is saving money. We all know how badly the nation is entrenched with poverty and illiteracy. However, there is always a way out with small measures being implemented. If we look at the issue, the nation has the capacity to save enough to actually bring down the fiscal deficit by almost 20 per cent, one-fifth rise in the income of those living below the poverty line, a 25 per cent increase in the expenditure on welfare or even catering to the hungry.

Everyone needs to realize that in order to save one does not have to spend. The logic is simple, this could be done if the usage of cash is reduced an instead, electronic transfers are used more often. This way, our country can save $23 billions, which means saving about a trillion rupees annually. Therefore there is a need to study how the electronic payments are changing the way of payments in India.

Sources of Data

The present study is based on the secondary data. This is gathered from the annual reports of RBI and different banks, published materials in the form of books, articles from journals, websites and reports relevant to the study. The study of electronic payments is changing the way of payments in India covers a period of nine years, commencing from 1st April, 2004 to 31st March, 2013.

Objectives of the Present Study

The objectives of the present study are:

1. To study the retail electronic payments by card types in India during 2004-05 to 2012-13;
2. To examine the growth of retail electronic payments in India during the study period.

Growth of Retail Electronic Payments by Card Types

India has been one of the fastest growing countries for payment cards in the Asia-Pacific region. About 35 per cent to 40 per cent of India's population is working with increasing disposable income year on year. Consumerism is set to add impetus to growth in the card base. In India there are two varieties of payment cards are available namely credit and debit cards. A credit card entitles its holder to buy goods and services based on the holder's promise to pay for these goods and services. The issuer of the card grants a line of credit to the consumer (user) from which the user can borrow money for payment to a merchant or to draw a cash in advance to meet the requirements of the user. A debit card provides an alternative payment method to pay in cash form at the time of purchases. It is also used for instant withdrawal of cash at Automated Teller Machines (ATMs). Debit cards also eliminate the risk of carrying cash. The following Table 1 presents the growth in retail electronic payments in terms of value by card types during 2005-06 to 2012-13 in India.

Table 1: Growth of Retail Electronic Payments by Card Types in India during 2005-06 to 2012-13

Years	Value (₹ billion)		Growth Rates	
	Credit Card	Debit Card	Credit Card	Debit Card
2004-05	256.86	53.61	—	—
2005-06	338.86	58.97	31.92	10.00
2006-07	413.61	81.72	22.06	38.58
2007-08	579.58	125.21	40.13	53.22
2008-09	653.56	185.47	12.76	48.13
2009-10	629.50	265.66	-3.68	43.24
2010-11	755.2	386.9	19.97	45.64
2011-12	966.1	534.3	27.93	38.10
2012-13	1229.5	743.4	27.26	39.14
Average			**22.29**	**39.50**

Source: Various Annual Reports of Reserve Bank of India.

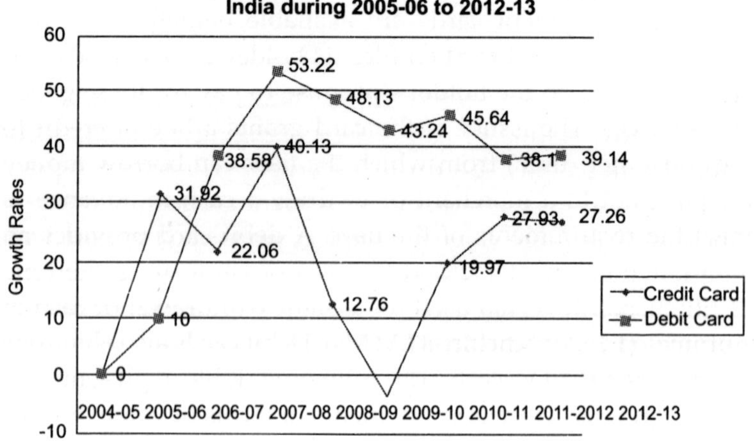

An examination of the above Table 1 reveals that the value of credit cards based transactions increased from ₹ 256.86 billion in the year 2005-06 to ₹ 1229.5 billion in the year 20012-13 registering an all around growth rate 22.29 per cent. Though credit card based payment transactions have been in India for over two decades now, only the last three years saw a real upswing in the market. Debit cards are the fastest growing card-based payment segment in India. Debit cards made their entry in India late 1998. Due to the nature of the product (buy now, pay now), it has experienced exponential growth. There is gradual increase in debit cards usage during the year when compared to previous years, though not in proportion to its growth in card base. The value of debit card based payment transactions grown from ₹ 53.61 billion in the year 2005-06 to ₹ 743.4 billion in the year 2012-13 registering an all around growth rate 39.50 per cent. It is also observed that the value of credit card payment transaction decreased in the year 2009-10 due to financial crisis.

Growth in Retail Electronic Payments in India

A retail payment system generally deals with low-value transactions made by bank customers. These are essentially the payments made from person-to-person, person-to-business, or person-to-government bodies. Retail and institutional customers now have a new way to transact, thanks to the technological advancement that has made e-payments a reality, over a period of time, proactively encouraging the introduction of electronic payment products that are superior to paper-based systems in terms of traceability, efficiency, speed and safety. These include large value payment options like the Real Time Gross Settlement (RTGS) as also retail payment options that facilitate multiple credit/debit transactions (Electronic Clearing Service (ECS)-credit/debit) or person-to-person electronic payments (NEFT). More Indian are now using retail electronic payments for several uses. The relevant data is presented in the following Table 2.

Table 2: Growth in Retail Electronic Payments in India during 2005-06 to 2012-13

(₹ billion)

Years	Electronic Clearing Services (ECS)				Growth Rates			
	ECS (Debit)	NECS/ECS (Credit)	Electronic Fund Transfer (EFT)/(NFET)	RTGS	ECS (Debit)	NECS/ECS (Credit)	Electronic Fund Transfer (EET)/(NFET)	RTGS
2004-05	29.21	201.8	546.01	40661.84	—	—	—	—
2005-06	129.86	323.24	612.88	115408.36	344.57	60.18	12.25	183.82
2006-07	254.51	832.73	774.46	184811.55	95.99	157.62	26.36	60.14
2007-08	489.37	782.22	1403.26	273183.30	92.28	-6.07	81.19	47.82
2008-09	669.76	974.87	2519.56	322798.81	36.86	24.63	79.55	18.16
2009-10	698.19	1178.33	4110.88	394533.59	4.24	20.87	63.16	22.22
2010-11	736.5	1816.9	9391.5	484872.3	5.49	54.19	128.45	22.90
2011-12	833.6	1837.8	17903.5	539307.5	13.18	1.15	90.64	11.23
2012-13	1083.10	1771.3	29022.4	676841.0	29.93	-3.62	62.10	25.50
Average					**77.82**	**38.62**	**67.96**	**48.97**

Source: Reserve Bank of India annual Reports 2009-10.

Growth in Retail Electronic payments in India during 2005-06 to 2012-13.

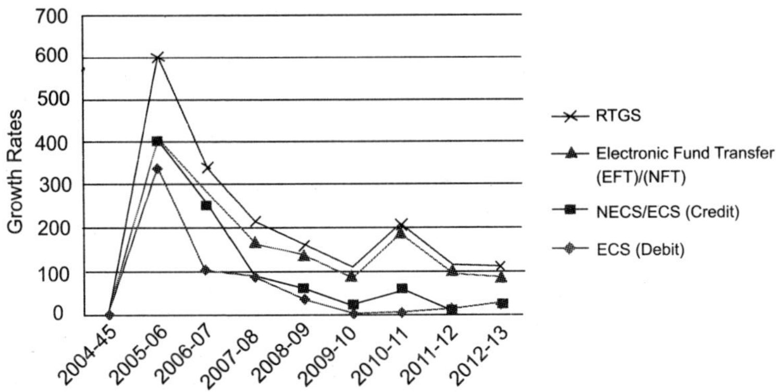

An examination of the above Table 2 reveals that the value of ECS (Debit) transactions increased from ₹ 29.21 billion in the year 2005-06 to ₹ 1083.10 billion in the year 20012-13 registering an average growth rate 77.82 per cent and ECS (Credit) transaction increased from ₹ 201.8 billion in the year 2005-06 to ₹ 1771.30 billion in the year 20012-13 registering an average growth rate 39.62 per cent. The value of ECS (Credit) transaction recorded negative growth rates in the year 2007-08 and 2012-13. The value of NEFT transactions increased from ₹ 546.01 billion in the year 2005-06 to ₹ 29022.40 billion in the year 20012-13 registering an average growth rate 62.10 per cent, There is gradual increase in ECS (Debit), ECS (Credit) and NEFT usage during the year when compared to previous years, though not in proportion to its growth in retial electronic payments. It is also observed that the value of NEFT transaction more increased than ECS (Debit) and ECS (Credit) transactions during the study period. This momentous growth rate indicating that the Indian retail payment system move to more advanced efficient and reliable systems comparable to global standards. There are so many advantage and reasons to the growth of retails electronic payments in India.

CONCLUSION

The Indian payment sector is witnessing a slow and gradual up and down change. It is steadily shifting towards electronic payment systems. However, the large geographic spread of locations and slow acceptance of the digitized payment mechanism by Indian are the major hindrances in this transition. Even in developed country's paper based payments still continue to coexist with advanced electronic payment systems. It is therefore can be concluded that paper-based payment mechanisms will continue to exist in the Indian market. One thing is certain; the current trends do herald the beginning of a new era in the country's payment systems, and new chapters in the history of payment systems in India will soon be written.

REFERENCES

Abrol, R.K. (1996), "Electronic Banking", IB A Bulletin, 18 (1), January, Mumbai.

Annual Reports of Reserve Bank of India (2005-2013).

Bellis M. 2003, The History of Money and Credit Cards.

www.rbi.org.in.

E-Banking Management
Edited by: Dr. Rabi N. Misra
ISBN: 978-93-5056-788-3
Edition: 2016
Published by: Discovery Publishing House Pvt. Ltd.,
New Delhi (India)

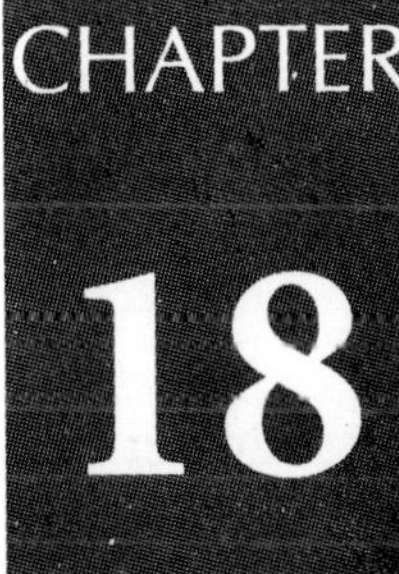

CHAPTER 18 Real Time Gross Settlement System —A Study

Dr. K. Kanaka Raju
Assistant Professor,
Department of Management Studies,
Andhra University

Introduction

This Real Time Gross Settlement System (hereinafter referred to as the RTGS System), set-up, operated and maintained by the Reserve Bank of India (RBI) comprises of the RTGS application, the Inter-Bank Funds Transfer Processor (IFTP) application and the RTGS Member (RTGS Participant) Interface application. The RTGS and the IFTP applications will, for the purposes of this document, be referred to as the Central System jointly. The Member Interface (hereinafter referred to as the PI) will be provided by the Reserve Bank of India (RBI) to all the Type 'A' and 'B' members of the RTGS System. These Operating Guidelines shall be called the Real Time Gross Settlement System and applicable time stamps involving the RBI and the RTGS members for all matters relating to the Central System.

Objectives of the Study

The study contains the following objectives:

- To know how to get a RTGS membership and detailed types of membership.
- To understand the technical mechanism of operating of settlement account and funding account.
- To extract the nature of transactions involved in Real Time Gross Settlement System
- To examine the Procedure for Communication between the PI and Central System
- To reveal the process of the Intra-day Liquidity (IDL) Facility.
- To know the process of RTGS Business.

RTGS Membership Type: Entities in the banking and financial sector in the country, on being granted RTGS membership, will each be assigned a membership type. The membership type of each RTGS member will determine the transaction types for which the RTGS member will be eligible under the RTGS System. The membership type will be assigned at the discretion of the RBI. Till notified otherwise, the RTGS members will fall into the following membership types.

Membership Type 'A': All the Scheduled Banks, including the Scheduled Cooperative Banks, will be eligible for Membership Type 'A'. All such RTGS members will be eligible for all types of RTGS Transactions including customer-based RTGS Transactions. Such a member will have a PI and eligible for Intra-day Liquidity.

Membership Type 'B': All the Primary Dealers will be eligible for Membership Type 'B'. All such RTGS members will be eligible for all types of RTGS transactions excluding customer-based RTGS transactions. Such a member will have a PI and eligible for Intra-day Liquidity.

Membership Type 'C': A bank or a Primary Dealer, operating in Call Money Market and maintaining one or more

Current Accounts in the Deposit Accounts Department, RBI, Mumbai, will be eligible for Membership Type 'C'. Such a member will neither have a PI nor will be eligible for Intra-day Liquidity and will avail of RTGS facilities only through Sponsor Banks.

Membership Type 'D': All the Clearing Entities, taking care of Net Settlement Clearings, will be eligible for Membership Type 'D'. Each such member will have a Net Settlement Interface software from the RBI. Each Type 'D' Member will be eligible to submit Multilateral Net Settlement Batche/s (MNSBs) to the Central System.

Settlement Account & Funding Account

1. All the RTGS Type 'A' and Type 'B' members will be eligible for a separate account each, called the 'Settlement Account' with the Deposit Accounts Department, RBI, Mumbai. This 'Settlement Account' will be opened by Bank for each such RTGS member on its admission as an RTGS member. The Settlement Account will be used exclusively for the purpose of the settlement of the RTGS transactions like Inter-institutional transactions, Customer transactions. Delivery versus Payment transactions and Own Account transfers Transactions.
2. Multilateral Net Settlement Batches (MNSB) Transactions. The eligibility of a RTGS member to undertake all or a subset of the above transaction types will be governed by its RTGS membership type.
3. The Settlement Account of each RTGS member will be funded at the RTGS Start-of-Day from the RTGS member's Funding account i.e. a Current Account maintained with the Deposit Accounts Department, RBI, Mumbai and designated as the Funding Account for the purpose by the RTGS member. The RTGS member will provide a duly authorized mandate, in the form of a Standing Instruction, in the prescribed format, in favour of RBI, Mumbai for debiting its current account and crediting its Settlement Account.

4. The mandate for funding the Settlement Account will indicate the funds, to be transferred from the Funding Account to the Settlement Account, at the RTGS Start-of-Day, One of the following options in this regard may be indicated by the RTGS member in this mandate:
   (*a*) **Amount:** The actual amount of funds to be transferred from the Funding Account to the Settlement Account.
   (*b*) **Residual Amount in the Funding Account:** The minimum amount, which must always remain in the Funding Account thereby making available funds above this amount in the Funding Account for transfer to the Settlement Account.
   (*c*) **Percentage of the Available Funds :** A specified percentage of the balance in the Funding Account for transfer to the Settlement Account.
   (*d*) **Percentage above Residual Amount:** A specified percentage of the balance, above a specified minimum amount in the Funding Account, will be transferred to be Settlement Account.
5. The RTGS Settlement Account of any member can start with a zero balance at the beginning of any RGTS business day.

Nature of Transactions: The following base transaction types will involve the respective Settlement Accounts/Current Accounts of the RTGS members:

(*a*) Inter-institutional Transactions.
(*b*) Customer Transactions.
(*c*) Delivery versus Payment Transactions.
(*d*) Own Account transfers Transactions.
(*e*) Multilateral Net Settlement Batches (MNSB) Transactions.

New Transaction Types : New transaction types can be defined by the Bank. Each transaction type may differ from the other transactions type(s), associated with the same base transaction type in respect of default priority, operating and settlement sessions and eligibility for Intra-day Liquidity.

Procedure for Communication between the PI and Central System

Each RTGS member with a PI will communicate with the Central System through the PI only:

1. **Mode of Communication**: The Indian Financial Network (INFINET) or any other communication network, as may be specified by the Bank for the purpose from time to time, will be the communication backbone for all such interactions.
2. **Security of Communication:** All the messages between the PI and the IFTP System will be digitally signed and encrypted for ensuring security of message transfer.
3. **Format for Communication:** All messages between the PI and the IFTP system will be exchanged only in the message formats, as specified in the User Guide, supplied to the RTGS members by the Bank and will not accept any other message format for processing.
4. **Unique Identification for Messages:** Every message, released by the PI to the IFTP system, will be assigned a Unique Transaction Reference (UTR) before it is released.
5. **Duplicate Handling:** If a message is received by the IFTP system with a UTR, which was received earlier and if the contents of the message are the same as that of the earlier message received from the PI, the message will be treated as a duplicate and will not be processed by the IFTP System.
6. **Sending Payment Messages to IFTP System:** An RTGS Member may send, *inter alia,* different kinds of payment messages (transactions) to the RTGS System through the IFTP System. Every message, received by the IFTP System, will be acknowledged by the IFTP System, after subjecting the message to a set of security, format and business validations. A positive IFTP acknowledgement will be sent to the PI originating the message, indicating that the message has been accepted for further processing.

7. **New Transaction Types:** Each new transaction type will be based on one of the base transaction types, specified herein and will be associated with the base transaction type through code words. Each transaction type may differ from the other transactions type(s), associated with the same base transaction type in respect of default priority, operating and settlement sessions and eligibility for Intra-day Liquidity.
8. **Priority of Transactions:** Each payment transaction, originating from a PI (except an MNSB) must be assigned a priority, before it can be taken up for settlement by the RTGS System. The same priority can be assigned to more than one transactions. In such cases such transactions shall be settled on the first-in-first-out basis.
9. **Settlement of Transactions:** A payment transaction is deemed to have been settled when the Settlement Account or the Current Account (of a Type 'C' member) of the RTGS member (which is to be debited through the transaction) has been debited and the Settlement Account (Current Account of a Type 'C' Member) of the RTGS member (who is to be credited through the transaction) has been credited. A transaction will be settled only if there is sufficient balance in the Settlement Account, On settlement of transactions, all the RTGS members, whose Settlement Accounts have been debited/credited, will be notified by the Central System, provided the RTGS members have a PI each.
10. **Multilateral Net Settlement Batches:** All MNSB transactions (arising out of Net Settlement Clearings of Type 'D' Members) will be settled through the RTGS System. These include net settlement batches arising from Cheque Clearing Operations, Foreign Exchange Clearings, Electronic Funds Transfer, Electronic Credit and Debit Clearings, Government Securities Clearings and any other MNSBs, as decided by the RBI from time to time.

11. **Un-cleared Funds Account:** Each RTGS member, which participates in a clearing settlement with associated returns or in a clearing settlement, which has an associated dishonor period, must designate an Un-cleared Funds Account, at the time of being granted the status of an RTGS member.
12. **Queuing Mechanism:** Unsettled payment transactions, if so configured by the member/or by default, will be maintained in the RTGS system in a logical Payment Queue, pending settlement. The queue will be ordered by priority numbers of the transactions and, within a priority number, by the time of receipt in the RTGS System. No transaction will be taken up for settlement unless it is at the top of the payment queue, though members may, by cancellation or re-prioritization of such unsettled transactions in the Payment Queue, change the order of the transactions waiting in the payment queue.
13. **Gridlock Mechanism :** The Bank may, at its sole discretion, invoke the gridlock resolution mechanism of the RTGS System to settle queued transactions at periodic intervals.

Intra-day Liquidity (IDL) Facility: The Bank may, at its sole discretion, grant access to intra-day liquidity (IDL) facility to the Type 'A' or 'B' members for the settlement of their RTGS transactions. The Bank will provide the intra-day liquidity facility to the eligible RTGS members to help overcome short-term requirements for funds (during the RTGS business day) for settlement of the transactions. *The eligible RTGS members will use the intra-day liquidity facility only for overcoming genuine short-term funds requirements* Only Type 'A' or Type 'B' members are eligible for IDL support from the Bank. Bank will determine the maximum IDL a member can avail of at any point of time. The limit may be increased or decreased by the Bank, at its sole discretion. All IDL, provided by the Bank, will be through a Repo transaction involving eligible securities. The securities, eligible for IDL include dated Central Government securities and Treasury Bills and any other securities, notified by the Bank for the purpose.

IDL will be granted to the eligible RTGS members by way of intra-day Repo.

Customer Transactions: Type 'A' members can send/ receive customer transactions on behalf of their customers. Customer transactions can be sent through the RTGS System at any time from the start of the RTGS Business Day till such time as decided by RTGS Standing Committee from time to time and notified to members in advance. Credit under customer transactions, received by the RTGS member in its Settlement Account through the RTGS System.

Controlling Transactions-Re-prioritization of Transactions: An RTGS member may change the priority of a payment transaction, originated by it, provided the transaction has not been settled or cancelled and the new priority is not within the range, as reserved for use by the Bank.

RTGS Business Day: Each RTGS Business Day will be divided into four business day phases, RTGS Open Phase, IDL Shut Phase, IDL Close Phase and RTGS EOD Phase: The RTGS Open Phase is that phase of the RTGS Business Day during which all normal transactions are accepted and processed by the RTGS system in consonance with the existing operating session restrictions. During the IDL Shut Phase, transactions are processed as during the RTGS Open Phase except that no new IDL will be available even for transactions which are otherwise eligible for IDL. Close Phase also with the further restriction that no transactions, which debit an RTGS member with outstanding IDL, will be settled.

Security: Each RTGS member shall ensure compliance with the procedures laid down by the Certifying Authority (*i.e.* IDRBT CA) in regard to the generation and use of the digital signatures and/or encryption/decryption methodologies, as required for participation in the RTGS System. The RTGS members shall also ensure compliance of any instructions issued relating to the , security, house keeping etc., issued from time to time by the Bank and follow the User Guide relating to the PI with regard to their participation in the RTGS System.

CONCLUSION AND SUGGESTIONS

This paper seeks to explain the process of Real Time Gross Settlement System, like RTGS Membership Type, Settlement Account & Funding Account, Nature of Transactions, Procedure for Communication between the PI and Central System, Sending Payment Messages to IFTP System, Intra-day Liquidity (IDL) Facility Re-prioritization of Transactions and security of this RTGS System. This Real Time Gross Settlement System (hereinafter referred to as the RTGS System), set up, operated and maintained by the Reserve Bank of India (RBI). All the Scheduled Banks, including the Scheduled Cooperative Banks, will be eligible for Membership Type 'A'. All the Primary Dealers will be eligible for Membership Type 'B'. A bank or a Primary Dealer, operating in Call Money Market and maintaining one or more Current Accounts in the Deposit Accounts Department, RBI, Mumbai, will be eligible for Membership Type 'C'. All the Clearing Entities, taking care of Net Settlement Clearings, will be eligible for Membership Type 'D'. This 'Settlement Account' will be opened by Reserve Bank for each such RTGS member on its admission as an RTGS member. The Settlement Account will be used exclusively for the purpose of the settlement of the RTGS transactions like Inter-institutional transactions, Customer transactions. Delivery versus Payment transactions and Own Account transfers Transactions and Multilateral Net Settlement Batches (MNSB) Transactions. Each RTGS member with a PI will communicate with the Central System through the PI only. An RTGS Member may send, *inter alia*, different kinds of payment messages (transactions) to the RTGS System through the IFTP System. The Bank will provide the intra-day liquidity facility to the eligible RTGS members to help overcome short-term requirements for funds (during the RTGS business day) for settlement of the transactions.. Each RTGS Business Day will be divided into four business day phases, i.e. RTGS Open Phase, IDL Shut Phase, IDL Close Phase and RTGS EOD Phase. Each RTGS member shall ensure compliance with the procedures laid down by the Certifying Authority (i.e. IDRBT CA) in regard to the generation and use of the digital signatures and/or encryption/decryption methodologies, as required for participation in the RTGS System. Hence, it is conclude that, this system overcomes the all hurdles and emerged as a successful mechanism for the Reserve Bank of India.

REFERENCES

Arbra, K. (2003). Indian Banking: Managing Transformation through IT. IBA Bulletin, Vol. 25, No. 3, pp. 134-138.

Harmeen Kaur and Sandhu, H. S. (2003). Impact of Information Technology on the Indian Banking Sector, (ed), Economic Reforms in India - From First to Second Generation and Beyond, New Delhi: Deep & Deep Publications.

Sunita Agrawall and Ankit Jain-Technological Advancement in Banking Sector in India: Challenges Ahead.

Utkarsh Tiwari—Innovations in Banking Sector in 21st century.

Index

F

G

J

K

L

M

N

O

P

R

S

T